Meeting Special Educational Ne... in Secondary Classrooms

There are greater numbers of children with special educational needs and disabilities (SEND) now attending mainstream schools. This fully updated and revised edition of *Meeting Special Educational Needs in Secondary Classrooms* is written by an experienced teacher, adviser and SEN consultant, and explains the challenges that these children face. This is a practical book full of guidance for teachers and teaching assistants who support children with SEND in mainstream secondary classrooms.

Now fully updated to include the requirements of the 2014 Children and Families Act and SEND Code of Practice, this book:

- covers all aspects of teaching children with SEND, including planning, teaching and learning;
- promotes successful communication between teachers, parents and pupils;
- contains photocopiable resources and templates.

With practical guidance on how to make the curriculum more accessible for children with SEND, this book will help teachers and TAs work together to support pupils with special educational needs and disabilities more effectively.

Sue Briggs is a nationally recognised expert in special educational needs and disabilities (SEND) and inclusion.

Meeting Special Educational Needs in Secondary Classrooms

Inclusion and how to do it

Second edition

Sue Briggs

Routledge
Taylor & Francis Group

LONDON AND NEW YORK

Second edition published 2016
by Routledge
2 Park Square, Milton Park, Abingdon, Oxon OX14 4RN

and by Routledge
711 Third Avenue, New York, NY 10017

Routledge is an imprint of the Taylor & Francis Group, an informa business

First published 2005 by David Fulton Publishers Ltd

British Library Cataloguing-in-Publication Data
A catalogue record for this book is available from the British Library

Library of Congress Cataloging-in-Publication Data
A catalog record has been requested

ISBN: 978-1-138-85441-3 (hbk)
ISBN: 978-1-138-85442-0 (pbk)
ISBN: 978-1-315-72112-5 (ebk)

Typeset in Galliard and Gill Sans
by Florence Production Ltd, Stoodleigh, Devon, UK

To Hannah, Jessica and Eleanor, my beloved and loving daughters

With especial thanks to my eldest daughter, Hannah Hall, for her expert contribution to the inclusive teaching and learning checklist.

Contents

Chapter 1

Introduction
Inclusion in the secondary school context

Inclusion looks different in every school. You need to find strategies that work for *your* subject team, in *your* classrooms with *your* pupils. Inclusion is not a fixed state – it's a process that takes time to achieve. Rather than sudden change, it is a process of continuous school improvement. Inclusion has to work for each individual subject teacher in each classroom. By finding out what works for you and by ditching what does not, you can celebrate and enjoy the triumphs and learn from strategies that turn out to be less successful. Teachers are not expected to put everything in place overnight, but they should begin to look for new ways of including children with a diverse range of needs. The ideas and suggestions that follow are intended to support school leaders, faculty team leaders, and subject teachers, as together they develop their own inclusive practice.

Throughout this book the term 'pupils with special educational needs and disabilities (SEND)' is used. A pupil has special educational needs if he or she:

- has a significantly greater difficulty in learning than the majority of others of the same age; or
- has a disability which prevents or hinders him or her from making use of facilities of a kind generally provided for others of the same age in mainstream schools or mainstream post-16 institutions.

The term 'parent' is used throughout and is intended to cover any additional main care-givers.

The legislative framework

The Children and Families Act 2014 introduced changes important for all teachers about the education and inclusion of pupils with special educational needs and disabilities. Part 3 of the Act heralded the first major revision of the SEN framework for thirty years. Central to Part 3 of the Act is Section 19. This section sets out the principles underpinning the legislation and outlines the expectations of local authorities, schools, and health and social care services. It is about how these organisations work with parents of children and young people with SEND. Section 19 states:

> In exercising a function under this Part in the case of a child or young person, a local authority in England must have regard to the following matters in particular –

(a) the views, wishes and feelings of the child and his or her parent, or the young person;

(b) the importance of the child and his or her parent, or the young person, participating as fully as possible in decisions relating to the exercise of the function concerned;

(c) the importance of the child and his or her parent, or the young person, being provided with the information and support necessary to enable participation in those decisions;

(d) the need to support the child and his or her parent, or the young person, in order to facilitate the development of the child or young person and to help him or her achieve the best possible educational and other outcomes.

(SEND Code of Practice, 2015, 1.1, p. 19)

This is a radical departure from how previously many statutory organisations have interacted with parents, and demands changes in organisational systems and culture, and professional attitudes towards children, young people and their families.

In addition to the clearer focus on the participation of children, young people and parents in decision making at individual and strategic levels, the other significant changes to the SEND framework include:

- for children and young people with more complex needs, a co-ordinated assessment process and Education, Health and Care (EHC) Plans replacing statements of special educational needs;
- a strong focus on higher aspirations for children and young people with SEND, and, rather than the previous focus on provision, on improving outcomes;
- an expectation of close co-operation between health, education and social care, including joint planning and commissioning of services;
- a duty on local authorities to have a Local Offer of the services ordinarily available for children and young people with SEND and their families;
- in schools, a single category of SEND (SEN Support), replacing School Action and School Action Plus;
- a 'best endeavours' duty on schools: schools must use their best endeavours to make sure that a child or young person with SEN gets the support he or she needs – this means doing everything they can to meet children and young people's SEN.

(SEND Code of Practice, 2015, 6.2, p. 92)

This best endeavours duty is a key duty for governing bodies and this legal duty is directly with them rather than the headteacher of the school, as governors are responsible for the appointment and performance management of school leaders. Importantly, the 'best endeavours' duty is proactive in that it requires the governing body to ensure that the school is making the special educational provision that pupils need – governors should be sure that this is really happening rather than simply taking the word of the headteacher or SENCO. The duty applies not only to those with an EHC plan, but to all children with SEN, and is an important legal safeguard for children without an EHC plan.

- schools are required to publish an SEN Information Report on their websites;
- the framework covers all children and young people with SEND from birth to age 25.

The Equality Act 2010

Sitting alongside the Children and Families Act 2014, the requirements of the Equality Act 2010 remain in place. This is especially important because many children and young people who have SEN may have a disability under the Equality Act. The definition of disability in the Equality Act is: 'a physical or mental impairment which has a long-term and substantial adverse effect on a person's ability to carry out normal day-to-day activities'.

'Long-term' is defined as lasting or being likely to last for 'a year or more', and 'substantial' is defined as 'more than minor or trivial'. The definition includes sensory impairments such as those affecting sight or hearing, and, just as crucially for schools, will include children with long-term health conditions such as asthma, diabetes, epilepsy, and cancer.

As the SEND Code of Practice (DfE, 2015, p. 16) states, this definition provides a relatively low threshold and includes more children than many may realise. Children and young people with some conditions do not necessarily have SEN, but there is often a significant overlap between disabled children and young people, and those with SEN. Where a disabled child or young person requires special educational provision, they also will be covered by the SEN definition.

This doesn't apply to our school. We don't have any disabled pupils. Oh yes, it does apply to your school. It applies to all schools, including academies and free schools, university technical colleges and studio schools, and also to further education colleges and sixth form colleges.

Importantly, the duties are anticipatory in that they cover not only current pupils but also prospective ones. Schools are required to have accessibility plans for disabled pupils that address three elements of planned improvements in access:

- improvements in access to the curriculum;
- physical improvements to increase access to education and associated services;
- improvements in the provision of information for disabled pupils in a range of formats.

Schools also have wider duties under the Equality Act to prevent discrimination, to promote equality of opportunity and to foster good relations. These duties should inform all aspects of school improvement planning from curriculum design through to anti-bullying policies and practice.

But we don't have the specialist knowledge for these pupils. As part of their diverse school communities, secondary schools have always welcomed pupils with a range of special educational needs and disabilities. But schools sometimes for a number of reasons can be reluctant to include a pupil with more significant or complex needs. These reasons may include a perceived lack of expertise, worries about behaviour and, most commonly expressed, concerns about the effect that pupil might have on the education of other pupils in that class.

The SEND Code of Practice is very clear that where the parent of a pupil with an EHC plan makes a request for a particular school, the local authority *must* comply with that preference and name the school in the plan unless:

- it would be unsuitable for the age, ability, aptitude or SEN of the child or young person, or

- the attendance of the child or young person there would be incompatible with the efficient education of others, or the efficient use of resources.

(SEND Code of Practice, 2015, 9.79, p. 172)

Equally, schools cannot refuse to admit a pupil who has SEN but who does not have an EHC plan because they do not feel able to cater for those needs, or because the child does not have an EHC plan.

Won't including a pupil with complex SEND mean more work for teachers, leaving less time for the other pupils? Isn't that incompatible with the efficient education of the other children? Undoubtedly, there will initially be more work for teachers, especially in preparation and training, but once systems have been set up (and provided the whole school is committed to inclusion), in a short time the pupil with SEND will become just another member of the year group. Under the Equality Act 2010 schools are required to make reasonable adjustments for pupils with a disability, and that the preparation and training necessary to include a particular pupil is deemed to be a reasonable adjustment.

Teachers and teaching assistants are enormously resourceful and creative people, with more skills and knowledge than they realise. Pupils with SEND are just that – pupils – and each has his or her individual talents, strengths and needs. A colleague once commented: 'It's all a mind game really, isn't it Sue?' – and she was right. Focus more on the pupil's abilities and his or her personality and less on the difficulties and 'needs', and you will find just how rewarding it can be to help a pupil with SEND to grow as a full member of the school community.

What is the responsible body for our school? The 'responsible body' for a maintained secondary school is usually the governing body, and for academies and free schools, the proprietor. The responsible body is responsible, and ultimately liable, for the actions of all employees and anyone working with the authority of the school, such as contractors or parent helpers.

Will a school always know that a pupil has a disability? It is not always obvious that a pupil has a disability. Such disabilities as autistic spectrum disorder, dyslexia or epilepsy may not be immediately obvious and, along with other 'hidden disabilities' may not be recognised or diagnosed before a pupil transfers to secondary school. This can be because the child is generally more supported in the primary context and may have had few changes of teacher and classroom.

Underachievement or behaviour difficulties might relate to an underlying physical or mental impairment which could be covered by the Equality Act. A responsible body would have difficulty claiming not to have known about a disability if, on the basis of the pupil's behaviour or underachievement, it might reasonably have been expected to know that a pupil was disabled.

Try to avoid making assumptions about pupils based on a diagnosis, or reports from professionals. Each pupil is different and will respond to each situation in his or her unique way. By all means find out about the pupil's condition, but look at the disability in the context of the child as an individual. The social model of disability sees the environment as the primary disabling factor, as opposed to the medical model that focuses on the individual child's needs and difficulties.

Schools should take an environment-interactive approach. Interventions need to be centred on adapting the educational context rather than on 'fixing' the individual child's needs. Where schools focus on adapting systems and teaching programmes rather than trying to force the pupil to adapt to the existing context, in terms of outcomes for the pupil the chances of success are far greater. For example:

Case study: Reuben

Reuben joined the school in Year 7 with a small cohort of children from his village primary school. Reuben has had difficulties with reading from his earliest days in primary school and at chronological age 12 years 6 months he has a reading age of 7 years 2 months. He has a tentative diagnosis of specific learning difficulties/dyslexia and is going through an Education, Health and Care (EHC) needs assessment that is expected to lead to an EHC plan.

Reuben's school originally planned to use the additional funding to appoint a teaching assistant for 15 hours each week to support him by sitting with him to 'differentiate' lessons. However, when the SENCO investigated the interventions that Reuben had experienced in primary he realised that he had never had specialist teaching to address his dyslexia. The SENCO then used the funding to buy in a specialist teacher to assess Reuben to find out the exact barriers to his progress in literacy and to work with him for an hour each week. The specialist teacher also met with Reuben's teachers and gave them strategies to support his reading and writing in lessons across the curriculum. In addition, the school instigated training for all staff on dyslexia friendly approaches and in time became a recognised 'dyslexia-friendly' school. These adjustments meant that not only did Reuben make excellent progress in literacy and all his subjects, but other pupils with literacy difficulties were also better supported and helped to make good or better progress.

The National Curriculum Inclusion Statement

The National Curriculum sets out the expectations of schools for the inclusion of all pupils; it includes those whose attainment is well above expected levels and those who have 'low levels of prior attainment or come from disadvantaged backgrounds'. The framework outlines how teachers can modify the curriculum as necessary in order to provide all pupils with relevant and appropriately challenging work at each stage of their education.

The National Curriculum Inclusion Statement reaffirms that teachers should have high expectations for all pupils and must plan lessons to ensure that barriers to achievement are overcome. The statement sets out two key principles of inclusion:

- setting suitable challenges; and
- responding to pupils' needs and overcoming potential barriers for individuals and groups of pupils.

(Department for Education, 2014, National Curriculum in England: framework document, p. 9)

Setting suitable challenges

The National Curriculum Programmes of Study set out what pupils should be taught and should learn in each school year. Within this framework all pupils ought to experience success and achieve their individual potential. Even though their individual potential may be different from others of the same age, pupils with SEND are no exception. To expect *all* pupils always to do the same work will ensure that some will find the work too easy, while for others the challenge will be about right: but there will remain a significant group in any class for whom the challenge is inappropriate and this group will fail. If failure occurs regularly, then pupils stop caring, begin to lack motivation, become disillusioned, and are likely to become disruptive.

Response to pupils' needs and the overcoming of potential barriers for individuals and groups of pupils

It is a teacher's responsibility to ensure that all pupils experience success and make good progress, and to modify learning activities and resources to that end is a test of their professional skills. Teachers must use a range of teaching strategies to match the diverse range of abilities in their classes. To plan appropriate activities it is possible to base work on the National Curriculum programmes of study from earlier or later years. The programmes of study for the year of the pupils' chronological age can be used as *contexts* for learning, and as starting points for planning learning experiences appropriate to a pupil's age and requirements. It is important for teachers to have high expectations, especially of pupils with more significant and complex learning difficulties. Such expectations will drive aspirational target setting, and encourage pupils to greater achievement. All pupils bring with them to school their own individual strengths and interests which influence the way in which they learn. In planning for diversity, teachers should be mindful of an individual pupil's experiences and motivations. The planning of approaches that allow pupils fully and effectively to take part in lessons will raise attainment for all and minimise disruptive behaviour.

What can teachers do to respond to pupils with diverse learning needs?

- *Create effective learning environments that help pupils develop motivation and concentration.* For some pupils this will mean an individual picture or symbol timetable or schedule to help them manage their time and resources, while other pupils may need an individual desk or workstation in order to be able to concentrate on their own work.
- *Plan appropriate activities that allow all pupils to experience success.* Design lessons that are interactive and which involve exploration and sensory activities. Ensure all pupils are able to succeed at their own level. Make sure all pupils and staff respect the achievements of others.
- *Use a range of teaching strategies to match individual learning preferences.* To help pupils who are not natural auditory learners provide additional cues, using pictures, film, objects, concept maps, or specialist software to help all pupils understand and retain important information.
- *Manage support for pupils, both in terms of staff, other pupils, and resources.* Think beyond one-to-one support for pupils with SEND, and investigate greater use of peer support or technology. Plan and adjust the style and level of support to develop

independence over time – a gradual withdrawal of direct support can be an important indicator of progress.

- *Use appropriate assessment approaches.* For some pupils with SEND, teachers ought to find ways of capturing small steps of progress. Use photographs, video, and samples of work as evidence over time of experience and progress. Equally important is the teacher's ability to be more analytical in assessment so as to inform planning. Diagnostic testing is an invaluable tool for the identification of exactly whatever is a barrier to learning, and which then allows the use of that information to find just the right evidence-based intervention.
- *Set suitable and achievable short-term targets for learning based on agreed outcomes.* Start with the pupil's long-term aspirations and use these as motivational contexts for learning. Then consider your subject outcomes for the next two or three years – usually up to the end of a key stage or phase. Identify the rate of progress necessary for the pupil to make good progress in that school year so as to achieve those outcomes, and devise short-term targets that are aspirational yet achieveable within a given period – usually about 12 weeks. Set targets with the pupils and, where possible, with their parents. Pupils should all be able to understand and aim at the targets, and be involved with them. By setting targets together with pupils and their parents, and giving the family strategies they can use at home to help their child succeed, you will maximise the pupil's chances of making really good progress.

Overcoming barriers to learning

There are many events and conditions in pupils' lives that create barriers to their learning: hunger, emotional upset, illness, family separation, bereavement, etc. For pupils with SEND, the barriers to learning may appear all too evident. However, some pupils with SEND will also be contending with additional barriers, such as a lack of sleep or family separation. It is important that teachers pick up the signs of these additional barriers and do all they can to support the pupil and his or her family.

Schools should be sure that inflexible systems and policies in the school do not create yet more barriers. Subject planning and assessment must take into account the type and extent of pupils' difficulties. For most pupils the need for curriculum access will be met through greater differentiation of tasks and materials. Some pupils with SEND will need access to more specialist equipment or approaches. These might include written materials in Braille or a screen reader for a pupil with a visual impairment, or the use of materials and resources that pupils can access through all the senses – sight, touch, sound, smell, taste.

Actions a school could take to help pupils overcome barriers to learning

- Provide help with communication, language and literacy. For example, to support communication, some pupils benefit from the use of key word signing, such as Makaton. Investigate how software such as Clicker 6 (Crick Software (www.cricksoft. com)) can support the development of literacy skills for individuals and groups. Use circle time activities to develop pupils' social use of language.
- Develop a pupil's understanding through all the available senses. Offer visual cues in lessons, or incorporate real-life artefacts and experiences.

- Plan for full participation in learning, including physical and practical activities; make plans to include an individual pupil with SEND, rather than as an afterthought, and plan lessons in which all the class can be involved.
- Help pupils manage their behaviour so that they may take part in learning effectively and safely. Structure lessons by using picture or symbol schedules. Provide a 'chill-out' table or area in the classroom. To prepare pupils for situations they are likely to find difficult, use pre-teaching or narratives.
- Help pupils manage their emotions, especially trauma and stress. Create opportunities for them to talk to a trusted adult or mentor. Using illustrated conversations and draw and write techniques, include the language of emotions in your teaching; these will help pupils learn how to manage their own emotions.

The National Curriculum Inclusion Statement stresses that 'lessons should be planned to ensure that there are no barriers to every pupil achieving. In many cases, such planning will mean that these pupils will be able to study the full national curriculum'(National Curriculum, framework document, 2014, p. 9).

Entitlement

Entitlement to the National Curriculum is very important for pupils with SEND, especially for children with severe and complex learning difficulties. Until 1944 these children were deemed to be ineducable and came within the responsibility of the national health system. Large numbers of children and adults with learning difficulties or disabilities were placed in long-stay hospitals and asylums. For years at a time children were separated from their families and local communities. Only in 1944 were local education authorities required to find out which children in their area had special educational needs and to make appropriate provision for them. From 1944 to 1970 children with severe learning difficulties were placed in training centres rather than schools, and had no access to qualified teachers. The Education (Handicapped Children) Act of 1970 meant that for the first time all children with disabilities were brought within the framework of special education, with an entitlement to be taught by qualified teachers. That path towards inclusion is part of the development of the entitlement for children with SEND to be taught with and alongside other children of the same age, and who do not have special educational needs. The entitlement of children and young people is not to be categorised by their disability. First and foremost they should be seen as children or young persons, and as learners. The question isn't whether there should be special schools, but how special and mainstream schools can together be facilitators of the wider inclusion process, to work together, to support each other, and to learn from each other for the benefit of all children and young people with SEND.

Welcoming pupils with SEND

You can make only one *first* impression, and that first impression is especially important for children and young people with SEND and their parents. Parents will be very sensitive to any negative comments or suggestions that their child might not fit in – comments such as: 'Have you visited the local special school? They have a wonderful hydrotherapy pool!'; 'We are a high-achieving school'; 'None of our teachers have specialist training' may be meant well but do not make the potential pupil or his or her parents feel welcome.

Just like all other parents, the parents of a pupil with SEND will want to know that their child will be safe and happy in the school, and that staff members are friendly and approachable. At a later date a talk with the SENCO can follow which will give parents information about the SEN provision available for all children, and will be an opportunity to discuss more individual issues.

When the parents of a child with SEND choose to entrust their precious son or daughter to your school, it should be taken as validation of the school's reputation and achievements. Give yourself permission to make mistakes along the way – don't get downhearted and blame the pupil with SEND for being there. Find a new strategy for one pupil and it will ease the way for another.

Clearing the ramp

One morning in January children arrive at school after a night of heavy snow. The caretaker is busy clearing snow away from the steps that lead to the temporary classroom. Peter, who uses a wheelchair, is very cold and asks the caretaker if he would clear the ramp so he can go into class. The caretaker tells him to wait because he must clear the steps for the others first, then he will clear the ramp. Peter's friend Kuli then suggests, 'But if you clear the ramp, we can all go in.'

Figure 1.1 Inclusion 'clears the ramp' for everyone (Giangreco, 2000)

Inclusive ethos and values – the ABC of inclusion

This book is principally about including pupils with SEND. In that context an inclusive ethos has three important strands:

- *Acceptance:* The school and local community accepts, welcomes, and values all children, young people and their families who live in that locality, no matter what language they speak, what disabilities they have, or what they do for a living.
- *Belonging:* A pupil's sense of belonging in the school community is a vital element of inclusion. Belonging is fostered by attitudes of staff and other pupils to individual difference and additional learning needs.
- *Community:* The school reflects, welcomes and serves the local area. It involves the people who live there, and accepts as its own all children and young people who live in that community. The whole-school community cares for and supports all pupils to enable them to succeed. Such support is a natural and important component of working at or attending the school.

Where schools successfully include pupils with SEND, the foundation of that success is the commitment of the headteacher and other senior staff to the broad principle of inclusion. The emphasis on inclusion is an impetus to raising standards for all pupils in the school. This impetus is underpinned by the wholehearted determination of all staff to work for the greatest possible success of all, and with a willingness to meet individual specific needs.

Inclusion as part of the school improvement process

Inclusion is about improving schools from both the academic and the social point of view. All too often inclusion is thought to be synonymous with special educational needs, but inclusion is a much wider concept than that. Inclusion is much more about making schools more humane and pleasant places in which to work and learn – for everyone. Inclusion is about making schools more responsive to the diverse needs of individuals and groups of pupils. There is a growing body of evidence to show that making schools more inclusive and more responsive to diverse needs actually drives up examination results. A school that is good for pupils with SEND is a good school for everyone.

What will Ofsted inspectors look for in terms of inclusion?

Inclusion is no longer a separate judgement in the Ofsted inspection framework. Rather, it is woven through all judgements as an expectation underpinning good practice and entitlement. Particularly important is the high priority given to the role of school leadership and management in developing an ethos of respect for diversity and in ensuring good outcomes for all pupils.

A part of all inspections is a focus on the effectiveness of leadership and management at all levels in creating a culture that fosters improvements in the school. This evaluates the extent to which the school meets the needs of the whole, often diverse, pupil population. In particular, inspection focuses on how effectively leadership and management at all levels promote improved teaching and how all pupils are enabled to overcome specific barriers to learning.

Ofsted investigates how a school's ethos develops awareness of and respect for diversity, including gender, race, religion and belief, culture, sexual orientation and disability. Inspectors will explore how a school tackles negative attitudes held towards people with SEND, and will acknowledge where successful schools celebrate and value the success of all pupils, in so doing fostering mutual respect and raising self-esteem.

Inspectors will search for evidence that the school's practice consistently reflects the highest expectations of staff and the highest aspirations for pupils, including those with SEND. Alongside these expectations and aspirations, inspectors will look for teaching that engages and includes all pupils, and which results in good or better learning and progress for pupils with SEND. Inspectors often ask for a small sample of case studies, including case studies of pupils with SEND, in order to evaluate the experiences and outcomes of particular individuals and groups.

Another high priority for Ofsted inspectors is how effectively schools deal with all forms of bullying and harassment, including bullying related to special educational needs and disability; this category will include discriminatory and derogatory language.

How can schools change attitudes and expectations?

Everyone brings with them to their work all kinds of past experiences, beliefs and values, and it is just the same for people working in schools. For some the very concept of children and young people with more significant and complex SEND being taught in mainstream schools challenges the status quo and their long-held beliefs and understandings. Teachers and teaching assistants can experience feelings of inadequacy in meeting these pupils' needs, and often hold a fear of the unknown. Teachers tell of their concerns about keeping discipline, about not being able to communicate, about pupils' personal care, about medication, about epilepsy . . . about a pupil who is so 'different'. These worries are natural and understandable, but they are not valid reasons for *exclusion*. By talking to parents and support services, or by putting suitable training in place, all concerns may be addressed and many problems resolved before a pupil arrives.

There have always been children and young people with SEND in mainstream secondary schools. Nowadays the difference is that many of the children have a wider range of special needs, and in some cases they may even look a little different. A pupil with Down's syndrome can be more able than a child without such an obvious learning difficulty, yet a placement in a mainstream school may be questioned before the pupil's true ability is understood. Teachers need to look beyond the disability and see the real child or young person inside. Focus on the pupil's learning strengths and needs rather than on a medical diagnosis, and use the diagnostic label as a signpost rather than as a dead end. These pupils have a great deal to offer our schools if only we can learn how to recognise and celebrate their gifts.

> When we plant an orchid we water it and feed it. If it begins to droop or wilt, we tend it more carefully. We don't blame the orchid.

Language and terminology

The whole area of special educational needs and disability is a minefield containing ever-changing acronyms and jargon: 'The SENCO and the EP liaised with a SALT about EHC outcomes for a pupil with ASD.' These terms are a form of shorthand, and are useful for professionals. Used without care they can be intimidating for parents and irritating for some teachers. They do not make clear either the pupil's needs or the school's intentions. They may serve to exclude and alienate parents, and can sometimes alienate professionals from other agencies.

The words we use when we talk about pupils with SEND have an impact on the children and young people and on how they are perceived and treated. There is a useful rule of thumb when trying to decide what to say or write, which is to make sure the pupil is not defined by their disability or special need. In a sentence, try to put the pupil first and the disability or special need second – for example, 'a pupil with autism', rather than 'an autistic pupil'.

Some words have negative connotations and are no longer in general use – a word such as 'handicapped' has its root in disabled people going 'cap in hand' for charity. Medical terms such as 'spastic', 'cretin' or 'cripple' were once commonly used to describe people with special needs or a disability, but are now seen as inappropriate, particularly as they are often used as terms of abuse.

In general, the phrase 'a person with special needs' is used, and this form of wording covers most eventualities. It is easy to become so interested in a pupil's particular syndrome that his or her individual personality is overlooked. A favourite recollection is when a teacher said in a meeting that his pupil was 'more David than Down's'. This meant that the pupil's character, individual experiences and support network were of far more importance than his medical diagnosis.

None of us is perfect; everyone is prone to a slip of the tongue, and it would be terrible if fear of using the wrong terminology discouraged adults from talking to or being involved with pupils with special educational needs or disabilities. These children and young people are called 'special' for a reason – we can all benefit from being with them and getting to know them better.

Training for staff and pupils

For many years there has been no specialist initial teacher training course in special educational needs and disabilities. All trainee teachers have some training for special needs, but often this is as little as a few hours of lectures as part of a one-year course. This level of knowledge does not prepare teachers adequately to work with the full range of pupils with SEND usually found in mainstream secondary schools, especially with those pupils having more severe and complex learning difficulties. It now falls to schools themselves to source and arrange training for all staff.

If successful inclusion is to be achieved, careful preparation for admission should be started well before the pupil arrives. All teachers and teaching assistants should have training on the particular needs of the pupils with SEND who are to join the school community, and should be given guidance on appropriate teaching methods, learning activities, and specialist or adapted materials.

Training ought to be offered at a variety of levels. This should include:

- *Training in disability awareness and the requirements of the Equality Act 2010.* This training will help staff to understand the issues relating to disability and diversity in society and in schools. It will support them in developing acceptance and an understanding of diversity among other pupils within the school.
- *General information for all staff, including non-teaching staff members.* This will include an overview of the pupil's particular strengths and needs, the learning and behaviour strategies used in the child's current primary or middle school, and any relevant health and safety issues. Developing a one-page profile is an ideal way of disseminating the important information about a pupil's learning preferences and needs to all staff, including supply teachers and specialists from SEN support or therapy teams.
- *Advice and guidance for subject teachers and teaching assistants on ways of differentiating and adapting lessons and resources.* This advice will come from a range of sources such as local authority support services, speech and language therapists, educational psychologists, physiotherapists and occupational therapists. The SEND Code of Practice 2015 states that:

> Schools may involve specialists at any point to advise them on early identification of SEN and effective support and interventions. A school should always involve a specialist where a pupil continues to make little or no progress or where they continue to work at levels substantially below those expected of pupils of a similar age despite evidence-based SEN support delivered by appropriately trained staff.
>
> (SEND Code of Practice, 2015, 6.59, p.102)

- *Specialist training to address a pupil's specific needs.* This training, for example, could include teaching all staff a few signs, how to use symbols or a communication aid, and/or administer medication.
- *Ongoing opportunities.* All teachers, teaching assistants, and other support staff will need regular opportunities for meeting with more experienced or skilled colleagues and the SENCO, the advisory teacher, or the educational psychologist, and to discuss successful strategies and plan for the future.

Training opportunities

A number of third-sector organisations offer training opportunities for teachers and other school staff across the whole range of SEND. A number of these opportunities have been developed and funded in response to the Children and Families Act 2014 and the resulting SEND Code of Practice. For most schools these opportunities provide training at the awareness and enhanced levels of training. Schools should ensure that all teachers have the basic awareness level of training to meet the needs of current and prospective pupils with SEND; and that those teachers and teaching assistants who work directly with a child with SEND have had training to an enhanced level of knowledge and skill; and that some teachers have access to specialist training about particular types of SEND.

The levels of training outlined in the SEND Code of Practice 2015 are:

- *Awareness*: to give a basic awareness of a particular type of SEN, appropriate for all staff who will come into contact with a child or young person with that type of SEN.

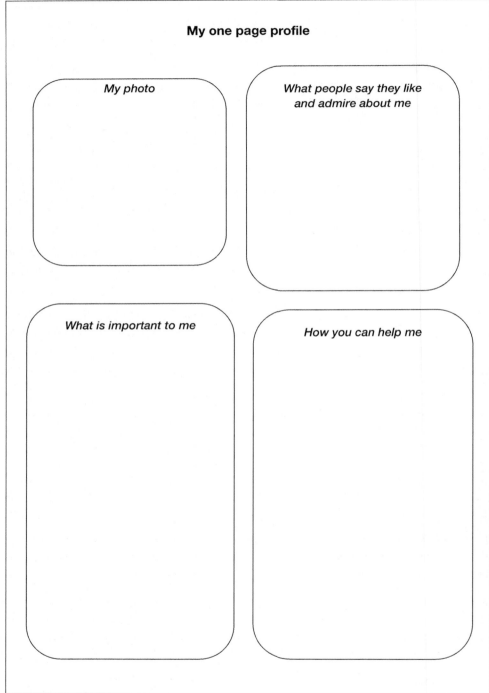

My one page profile

My photo

What people say they like and admire about me

What is important to me

How you can help me

Figure 1.2 My one-page profile

© 2016 *Meeting Special Educational Needs in Secondary Classrooms*, Sue Briggs, Routledge

- *Enhanced*:   how to adapt teaching and learning to meet a particular type of SEN, for early years practitioners, class and subject teachers and teaching assistants working directly with the child or young person on a regular basis.
- *Specialist*:   in-depth training about a particular type of SEN, for those staff who will be advising and supporting those with enhanced-level skills and knowledge.

(SEND Code of Practice, 2015, 4.32, p. 69)

It is vital that subject teachers have access to enhanced and specialist training, because this training will build on their existing pedagogic knowledge and skills. In too many schools training at all levels on SEND has only been offered to or accessed by teaching assistants, perpetuating the mistaken belief that they hold responsibility for pupils with SEND. The SEND Code of Practice (2015) underscores the fact that the subject teacher is responsible for the learning and behaviour of all pupils in their classes even when a pupil has full-time one-to-one support. 'Teachers are responsible and accountable for the progress and development of the pupils in their class, including where pupils access support from teaching assistants or specialist staff' (SEND Code of Practice, 2015, 6.36, p. 99).

Liaison with primary schools

This is a vital aspect of the secondary school's responsibilities in terms of general forward planning for all pupils. It is especially so for children and young people with special educational needs. Regular meetings with feeder primary schools will give a secondary school several years' advance knowledge of potential pupils. This means that any issues of both physical access and access to the curriculum can be addressed in good time. Use of common assessment criteria across families of schools will give a clear and shared understanding of the abilities and needs of the pupils, and provide a basis for planning appropriate teaching and learning strategies on transfer into Year 7.

Not why, but how?

Governments at both national and local level have made the inclusion of pupils with SEND into a political football. The reality is that these children are already in our mainstream secondary schools. Legislation – and a forest of books – have addressed the 'why' question about inclusion. This book sets out to give schools some help with the 'how'.

Chapter 2 looks at how mainstream secondary schools can prepare to welcome and include pupils with learning difficulties.

Understanding SEN Support and Education, Health and Care plans

Changes to the SEN system

The reforms to the SEN system introduced in 2014 include a radical restructure of the way provision in secondary schools is made for children and young people with SEND. From September 2014 only *one* category of special educational needs is used in schools. Known as SEN Support, this change is at the heart of the SEND reforms, and provides a strong focus to help pupils overcome as early as possible barriers to learning and achievement. No longer do pupils need to be seen to fail before they are moved to the next 'level' at which advice and support from external specialists can be brought in. Schools are free to ask for specialist advice and support as soon as there is a concern about a pupil's progress or development, and that advice is then available to form part of the decision-making process as to whether or not a pupil needs special educational provision. In this way as early as possible, and so as to close the gap between themselves and other pupils of the same age, pupils' strengths and needs can be identified, and more targeted support and interventions implemented to help them make accelerated progress.

The changes are set also in the context of the 'best endeavours' duty placed on school governing bodies by the Children and Families Act 2014. Here governors are required to use their best endeavours to secure the special educational provision called for by all pupils' special educational needs, not only for those with EHC plans.

For mainstream schools a further and major change in the SEND reforms is that of the importance and responsibility of the subject teacher for the progress of all the pupils in his or her class; and these responsibilities are acknowledged and emphasised. Thus, the subject teacher becomes the lynchpin of special educational provision; and it is the subject teacher who must manage and evaluate that provision, whoever delivers interventions or supports the learning of a pupil with SEND. No longer is anyone 'just a physics or maths teacher' – all teachers are teachers of SEND. 'Teachers are responsible and accountable for the progress and development of the pupils in their class, including where pupils access support from teaching assistants' (SEND Code of Practice, 2015, 6.36, p. 99).

What does this mean for SENCOs?

The SEND reforms also herald a shift in the role of and the expectations upon the SENCO. This key professional takes on a strategic and advisory role, as opposed to the more traditional direct SEN teaching. Chapter 6 of the SEND Code of Practice outlines this strategic responsibility of the SENCO for SEN policy, and includes the expectation that the SENCO, in order to meet pupils' needs effectively, will advise the governing body on the deployment of the school's delegated budget and other resources. This is a real step forward for SENCOs in terms of their increasing professionalism and high level of training and expertise. Development of the SENCO role also brings challenges to school leaders; to include SENCOs in school leadership teams and relinquish information about and control over the SEN budget. Without this status and responsibility SENCOs cannot be effective in a wider strategic role.

Freed from so much direct teaching, SENCOs can now focus on supporting colleagues who are less experienced such as newly qualified teachers, and develop the skills of subject teachers to meet a diverse range of abilities and needs. The SENCO will now be the leader of training for SEND in secondary schools, either delivering the training themselves or arranging experts to work with teachers across the school or across a group of schools. This allows SENCOs a profound influence both on the professional development of teachers and support staff, and an improvement in the quality of teaching and learning for all pupils in the school, including those with SEND.

Aspirations and outcomes

Another significant change to the SEN framework is the move away from simply identifying and meeting pupils' needs, to establishing what are the pupil's aspirations for the future and the outcomes they need to achieve in the following two or three years in order to reach those aspirations. This shift in emphasis allows the pupil's 'needs' to be seen as barriers to the achievement of outcomes – the things that get in the way – and allows objectives and targets to be set in the context of this longer view. We teachers have often focused on the 'next small step' when setting targets for pupils with SEND rather than thinking how and if that target will enable them to achieve the best possible outcomes for their future – living independently, having a job, a social life, relationships, etc.

Identifying special educational needs

The definition of special educational needs in the 2015 SEND Code of Practice is exactly the same as under the previous legislation – that is, a child or young person has special educational needs if he or she has a learning difficulty or disability which calls for special educational provision to be made for him or her. A child or young person has a learning difficulty or disability if he or she:

- has a significantly greater difficulty in learning than the majority of others of the same age, or
- has a disability which prevents or hinders him or her from making use of facilities of a kind generally provided for others of the same age in mainstream schools.

(SEND Code of Practice, 2015, pp. 15–16)

This definition of special educational needs has two parts, and a pupil must fulfil both parts before he or she can be identified as having special educational needs. Specifically, the pupil must have a learning difficulty or disability *and* require special educational provision to be made for him or her.

Before identifying children with SEND, it is crucial that teachers and SENCOs understand this definition and what constitutes special educational provision. Without such understanding pupils may well be identified as having SEND when the reason they have fallen behind other children is because of poor quality teaching. As part of all school inspections Ofsted inspectors will investigate that the processes for identifying SEND are sufficiently robust: 'They (inspectors) should find out whether pupils have been identified as having special educational needs, when in fact their progress has been hampered by weak teaching' (*School Inspection Handbook*, Ofsted, September 2014, p. 70).

A whole-school approach to identifying special educational needs

Just as every teacher is a teacher of SEND, so the accurate identification of pupils as having SEND is a whole-school job, and to be truly effective requires a whole-school approach. This has to be an integral part of the school's overall approach to the monitoring and tracking of pupils' progress and development, including the assessment of pupils' skills and level of attainment on entry. Inevitably this means that headteachers and governors must give a high priority to SEND, and communicate that priority to all teachers and support staff. A strong and inclusive vision clearly articulated by senior leaders and shared by all is the bedrock of good assessment and provision for SEND and of good outcomes for all pupils.

The key questions that school leaders must address are:

- How effectively do we listen to and work in real partnership with pupils and their parents?
- Are we able to identify barriers to learning as early as possible?
- Do we have the necessary assessment systems and expertise to support accurate identification of SEND?
- In identifying pupils' precise special educational needs how effective are the assessments we make when pupils enter the school?
- To support assessment and identification, do we make good use of external specialists, including colleagues from health?
- For children who experience barriers to learning before they join the school, how effective is our liaison with primary schools?

Although there is no longer a requirement for schools to maintain a formal register of special educational needs, most schools have a record of those pupils who have been identified with SEND. It is good practice to review this list or register at least once a year, and to be sure that the pupils actually do meet the criteria for SEND. This review will confirm that teachers are clear about the difference between pupils with SEND and those who are underachieving for other reasons. The review is also an opportunity to remove from the record those pupils for whom the SEN provision has been successful and whose needs can now be met by high quality, well-differentiated teaching.

The four areas of need

The SEND Code of Practice redefines the four broad areas of need. These are:

- communication and interaction;
- cognition and learning;
- social, emotional and mental health;
- sensory and/or physical.

Of course, pupils' needs do not fit neatly into these four broad areas, and many pupils will have needs spanning more than one area. Some children and young people with complex SEND will have needs across all the areas. The broad areas of need are therefore only a guide – a shorthand for professionals – and each pupil's unique and individual strengths, difficulties and needs must be considered as a whole.

Communication and interaction

Communication needs are those that hamper a pupil's ability to communicate effectively with other people. These needs are known as speech, language and communication needs (SLCN). SLCN might result in pupils having difficulties in saying what they wish to, such as with articulation difficulties, or stammering. Other pupils with SLCN will have difficulty understanding what is said to them, or experience difficulty in developing a full understanding and use of the social rules of communication. In school, the effect of these difficulties might be that a pupil may have little variety in his or her use of language, or may speak or write in a disorganised way.

Children and young people with an autistic spectrum disorder (ASD), which includes Asperger's syndrome, often have particular difficulties with social interaction, as well as with communication. These difficulties might be evident in pupils' social use of language – for example, they might say inappropriate or unrelated things in conversations. Children and young people with ASD also often have difficulties in using imagination, and may have a particular and narrow range of interests.

Cognition and learning

The cognition and learning area of need covers a wide range of learning difficulties from moderate difficulties principally affecting memory, literacy and numeracy, through to severe and complex learning difficulties that call for a sensory-based curriculum.

Social, emotional and mental health difficulties

This area of need includes a wide range of social and emotional difficulties which are faced by pupils in secondary schools, and which present in many different ways. Some pupils may display challenging and aggressive behaviour, while others will be or will become quiet and withdrawn. Schools should be alert to any potential mental health difficulties that could be the underlying cause of these behaviours. Mental health difficulties include depression and anxiety disorders, conditions that are often missed in children in primary schools (and which may only be identified following entry to secondary education). Equally, behaviours may reflect more significant conditions such as attention deficit hyperactive disorder, or an attachment disorder. By removing the term 'behaviour difficulties' from this area of need the Code of Practice signals a real change of focus away from the behaviour itself, and points towards the underlying difficulties or conditions of which the behaviour is a symptom.

The emphasis now is on secondary schools providing emotionally secure environments, free from bullying, and where support is available for those children, young people and their families who may have difficulties. For teachers and other staff this is likely to involve training to identify when pupils display signs of anxiety, or show social and emotional problems. For some pupils the social and emotional difficulties might be caused by a family crisis, such as divorce, a sibling going into hospital, or the death of a grandparent. Others will have social and emotional difficulties linked to attachment disorders, or to frequent changes such as in in foster care. As soon as the school has a concern, at an early stage the SENCO or form tutor should discuss any problems with parents or carers, and together a plan can be developed, involving external specialists where necessary. Schools will also be hugely influential in preventing mental health difficulties by planning activities across the curriculum specifically to help pupils develop social and emotional skills, and promoting their well-being and resilience.

Sensory and/or physical needs

Some children and young people need special educational provision because they have a disability which prevents or hinders them from making use of the educational facilities generally provided (SEND Code of Practice, 2015, p. 16). These needs include physical disabilities, visual impairment (VI), hearing impairment (HI) or a multisensory impairment (MSI). Children and young people with an MSI have a combination of vision and hearing difficulties.

Identifying the needs of individual pupils

It is you, the subject teacher, who is the most likely person to notice the point at which one of your pupils starts to fall behind, or finds some areas of learning increasingly difficult. Even if you think another teacher will have raised this and discussed the pupil with the SENCO, each teacher is responsible for doing everything they can to ensure a pupil gets the support he or she needs. It is always worth talking to the pupil's parents as soon as possible to check if something has changed at home. Check out your thinking with the school SENCO and discuss ways that can help the pupil get back on track.

Once you and the SENCO are confident that the quality of teaching across the curriculum is good, and there is no obvious other reason for the pupil's apparent learning difficulties, establish together a clear analysis of the pupil's needs. To do this you can draw on a range of sources including:

- your own and other subject teachers' assessments and experience of the pupil (are the pupil's difficulties evident in all subjects?);
- information from parents, including their views and experience of their child's progress and development;
- data about progress and attainment, including progress in developing social skills and friendships;
- the child's development in comparison to other children of the same age;

- the child's views about his or her learning;
- any advice and assessment from external specialist teachers or other professionals.

Involving the pupil and parents in identifying SEND

An early and vital part of the process of identifying SEND is to speak to the pupil and his or her parents or carers. It is not enough to inform them once a decision has been made; they must be involved as soon as you have concerns, and should be included in decisions about who to involve in more specialist assessments. Parents in particular hold key information about their child's early life and development, and this information often will help to pinpoint the exact nature of a pupil's barriers to learning and progress. Chapter 7 includes practical ideas and suggestions about how you can communicate effectively with pupils with SEND and find out their aspirations and feelings about their learning.

Special educational provision: 'additional to or different from'

Provision for special educational needs includes those interventions and supports that are additional to or different from the provision made generally for other pupils of the same age. High quality, well-differentiated teaching that is targeted at a pupil's particular learning needs is not special educational provision. This is the entitlement of all pupils in any class, and a school's first response to a pupil falling behind should be to check the quality of teaching across the curriculum. It is the quality of the day-to-day teaching that he or she receives that has the most effect on achievement, no matter how many interventions or how many hours of teaching assistant support a pupil with SEND is given. 'Special educational provision is underpinned by high quality teaching and is compromised by anything less' (SEND Code of Practice, 2015, 1.24, p. 25).

The Teachers' Standard (revised in 2013) number 5, 'Adapt teaching to respond to the strengths and needs of all pupils', underlines the importance of high quality class teaching for all, with the requirement that 'teachers must know when and how to differentiate appropriately, using approaches which enable pupils to be taught effectively' (Teachers' Standards: Guidance for school leaders, school staff and governing bodies, 2013, Department for Education London, p.11).

Special educational provision does not include those targeted booster schemes or programmes designed for pupils who need a little short-term help to reach national expectations. Schools are expected to make available these targeted programmes as part of the provision for all children and young people.

What 'special educational provision' describes is those specialist interventions or support designed for individuals or small groups who have been identified as having special educational needs. This includes additional support from specialist teachers – whether sourced from within the school staff or from external agencies – and teaching assistants, plus the specifically designed interventions tailored to pupils' areas of weakness, or to help them to make accelerated or sustained progress. It is this 'accelerated or sustained progress' that indicates whether or not an intervention is effective, and it is the impact of interventions and support that Ofsted inspectors will look for during inspections.' Inspectors should note whether pupils who receive additional interventions are demonstrating accelerated or sustained progress – this would indicate whether the intervention is effective' (School Inspection Handbook, Ofsted, September 2014, p. 70).

Special educational provision does not replace a pupil's entitlement to high quality, well-differentiated subject teaching. Rather, it builds on the firm foundation of this entitlement so that achievement and attainment gaps can be narrowed or closed. Some pupils with SEND may well access targeted provision in addition to special educational provision. For example, a pupil with a communication difficulty in a Year 8 class will have access to the whole-class subject teaching and learning activities across the curriculum. This should include activities to support his or her communication, such as a communication-friendly environment, circle time activities, talk partners, a visual timetable, auditory and visual games, and frameworks for written work. These activities are not special educational provision, but are part of the general differentiated activities and resources that should be available in all lessons – part of the universal provision. In addition, the same pupil may participate in some small group interventions – such as a booster phonics or social use of language group – not as a special educational provision but as part of the targeted provision for some pupils to help them reach age-appropriate expectations. The pupil also has a programme devised and monitored by a speech and language therapist. This programme is delivered by a trained teaching assistant and is part of the school's special educational provision.

Withdrawal from lessons for interventions

There are a number of important questions that teachers should answer before making decisions about whether interventions can be delivered outside the classroom but within lesson time. These questions are:

- Will the learning in the intervention be of greater value to the pupil with SEND than the teaching and learning that would take place in the classroom?
- Could the intervention or support be delivered as part of and located in the whole-class lesson or at another time, such as during the lunch break or immediately before school?
- What would the pupil be missing during the period of the withdrawal, both in terms of curriculum content and learning activities?
- Will there be an opportunity for the pupil to access both the curriculum content and the teaching that he or she has missed as a result of the withdrawal?
- Will the pupil have opportunities to generalise into whole class learning and activities what he or she has learned during the intervention?

Teachers must evaluate carefully whether the benefits of an intervention delivered outside the classroom outweigh those of him or her staying within the class. Remember that differentiated teaching targeted at the particular strengths and needs of all pupils in the class should be the norm: provision for SEND is additional, and must enhance rather than detract from that normal entitlement of high quality teaching. Whenever there is consideration to deliver interventions outside the classroom, parents and the pupil should be helped to understand the rationale behind it and they must be involved in the decision. As the Teachers' Standards make clear, teachers must 'communicate effectively with parents with regard to pupils' achievements and well-being' (Teachers' Standards, 2013, p. 13).

Record of Interventions   Class/Year:

Broad area of need	All pupils *Universal*	Plus for some pupils *Targeted*	Plus for a few pupils *Specialist*
Cognition and learning			
Communication and interaction			
Social, emotional and mental health difficulties			
Sensory and/or physical needs			

Figure 2.1 Record of interventions by area of need

The graduated approach

Once teachers, SENCO and parents are confident and in agreement with the identification of SEND, then action should be taken to remove barriers to learning and for the planning and implementation of special educational provision for the pupil.

SEN Support is based on a four-stage cycle known as the graduated approach. Four stages – *assess, plan, do and review* – form the process by which decisions and actions are continuously revisited, refined and revised. So teachers and parents develop a deeper understanding of the pupil's needs, and of what helps him or her to make good progress and achieve good outcomes. Although the Code of Practice refers to the graduated approach as a cycle, in practice it is more likely to be a spiral process through which, to help the pupil overcome barriers to learning and achievement, the teacher uses increasingly deep and detailed assessments to identify and plan interventions and support.

Within (and during) this spiral process the teacher and SENCO will develop a deep and more refined understanding of the pupil's needs, and of what helps him or her make accelerated progress and achieve good outcomes. As always, this graduated approach is underpinned by an entitlement for all pupils to have access to consistently high quality teaching. There is also an expectation that, alongside pupils who do not have SEN, pupils with SEND will engage in the activities of the school. These activities include learning activities in classrooms, extra-curricular clubs and sports, school social activities, and school trips, including those to other countries such as to the First World War battlefields.

Assess

Assessment is the starting point for identifying when a pupil may have a special educational need; regular on-going assessment of progress and the impact of any provision is also crucial. Initial assessments are likely to be made using the school's own systems, but as you work through a number of cycles of the graduated approach, it may be necessary to drill down into finer detail to pinpoint the individual's precise barriers to learning. You can then refine interventions and other provision and support accordingly.

A significant aspect within the reforms is that schools do not have to wait for pupils to fail before asking for advice from external agencies. This means that teachers are able to base their choice of support and interventions on accurate assessments and expert advice.

Questions that school leaders and SENCOs need to consider are:

- Do class teachers make effective use of a range of assessment tools to identify pupils' gaps and barriers to learning, and adapt their core teaching in the light of these findings?
- Does the school make effective use of advice and support from an appropriate range of external specialists to support assessment and identification of SEN?
- Does the school need to offer additional training to staff on areas of SEN in order to improve assessment and identification?

Plan

The planning stage of the graduated approach involves close co-operation and co-production with parents, the pupil, and any support staff who work with a pupil. Planning should include a number of components:

- Agreement of short- or medium-term learning targets for the following 6 or 12 weeks. These targets should be linked to and support the pupil's achievement of longer term outcomes and aspirations, and will be the means by which the effectiveness of the special educational provision is measured.
- Planning for any additional differentiation of the whole-class teaching, or training for the teacher or support staff, such as the organisation of the classroom, or the development of communication-friendly learning environments.
- Identification of the 'additional and different' provision that is to be put in place to enable the pupil to meet his or her targets. This will include targeted interventions, resources and support from specialist teachers or other support staff.
- Identification of any additional support or advice necessary from health or social care, such as a speech and language therapist or guidance from the Child and Adolescent Mental Health Service (CAMHS).
- Agreement of what parents can do at home to support their child's learning and progress, and how school will support them to do this effectively.
- Identification of what provision is available through the local authority 'Local Offer' to support the pupil and his or her family. The Local Offer sets out the provision the local authority expects to be available across education, health and social care for children and young people in their area who have SEND, including those who do not have Education, Health and Care (EHC) plans. The provision identified at this planning stage could be a youth club, a Scout group, a social group for young people with a particular SEND, or an 'autism-friendly' film screening at the local cinema.
- Establishment of an agreed date for review.

Before starting any intervention you should have a clear idea of what you want the impact of that intervention to be – you need to have a hypothesis against which you can assess progress. Wherever possible, introduce interventions one at a time. In this way you will be able to measure the impact of individual interventions. Having a number of interventions running concurrently makes it is impossible to know which one is making what difference, and could lead to the pupil missing out on whole-class teaching and activities.

Do

The 'do' section of the graduated approach is where you implement the additional or different interventions and support that have been planned and agreed with parents and the pupil. The number and frequency of interventions should not interfere with the pupil's access to high quality teaching and the full range of classroom experiences.

This implementation phase should last no longer than twelve weeks in any one cycle and ideally the impact of the interventions or support will be reviewed after about six weeks. This allows for the programmes and support to be adjusted for maximum impact on the pupil's learning and progress.

Whoever is leading the intervention will need carefully to record the pupil's responses to the intervention activities; and to note all evidence of learning so that the subject teacher at all times has an up-to-date picture of the child's progress. Even when a specialist teacher is leading an intervention, it remains the responsibility of the subject teacher to monitor the *impact* of the intervention. The story of Jerome is an example.

Jerome is in Year 8. He has particular difficulties with reading and writing and his provision includes twice-weekly additional small group interventions to improve his reading and spelling. These interventions are led by a trained teaching assistant under the supervision of Cathy, Jerome's English teacher. The teaching assistant notes Jerome's progress against the targets agreed with Jerome and his parents, and feeds back to Cathy each week so that she is aware of how Jerome is progressing and in order to maintain impact can make adjustments to the interventions.

Review

The clear expectation in the SEND Code of Practice is that a teacher – either the relevant subject teacher, form tutor or SENCO – will meet the parents of pupils with SEND at least three times each year to review progress and to discuss any issues that have arisen in school or at home. The SEND review meeting is the opportunity for teachers and parents together to review progress against learning targets, and to formulate new targets for the next twelve weeks. It is at this meeting that any new or additional assessments that might become necessary can be discussed. These more diagnostic assessments could be to identify a particular gap in learning, or to inform the choice of a more specialist evidence-based intervention. And so the cycle resumes.

The most positive outcome of SEN Support is that the pupil no longer needs to be identified with SEND, because he or she has made such good progress as a result of the SEND provision that the usual, high-quality differentiated class teaching will meet needs. This is what success really looks like.

Tips for good quality SEN Support

1 *Ensure all teaching and learning is of a high quality.* Access every day to good quality well-differentiated teaching is the key to improved outcomes for all pupils, including those with SEND. Investment in high quality professional development for teachers and support staff, and a relevant and creative curriculum that addresses the needs of all learners, will improve the learning and progress of all.

2 *Develop diagnostic tools and skills to assess precisely a pupil's individual learning needs and barriers to learning.* In order to be able to choose the most appropriate intervention (i.e. one that is likely to have a positive impact on outcomes), pupil's needs must be pinpointed precisely. If the skills or the diagnostic assessment tools are not available in school, then to do this you should commission the appropriate external professional such as a speech and language therapist, or an educational psychologist. Only when you know what exactly are the pupil's learning challenges can you begin to match the most appropriate and effective intervention for that individual.

3 *Investigate and use interventions that are well evidenced.* A number of organisations, including the Sutton Trust and the Communication Trust, have commissioned research into effective interventions and have the resulting information available on 'What works?' areas of their websites. This means that teachers are able to identify and use interventions that have a proven track record of success for a particular learning need.

Knowing what works and what doesn't is crucial, and you may need to look beyond mere progress data and include other key indicators to obtain a full picture of the impact of special educational provision. This process will include assessments which look for changes in attitude, behaviour, attendance and participation.

4   *Listen to and work with pupils and parents.* Parents of children with SEND invest an enormous amount of trust in their children's schools – trust that their children will receive good quality teaching and the appropriate provision for their learning and other needs. It can sometimes be difficult to live up to that trust, but, as discussed in Chapter 3, it starts with transparent and honest communication. The listening conversations that teachers have with parents and pupils are key to developing and consolidating that trust. And where pupils are given the opportunity to have a voice in planning their own learning, they are more likely to be motivated to try their best, even when they find concepts particularly difficult.

5   *Have a system for managing and co-ordinating provision, including SEN provision.* To make the best use of skills and resources, it is important that provision for SEND is managed right across the school. Most schools now use provision maps to co-ordinate all provision in school, including provision for pupils with SEND.

A comprehensive provision map will enable subject teachers to be clear about the whole range of provision that each pupil is receiving and SENCOs to have an overview across the school. A robust provision map also helps the SENCO to manage support staff more effectively, not only to know which pupils they are supporting and what they are doing, but also how effective that support is in accelerating progress and increasing independence. The provision map will underpin effective management across the school. A template for a provision map by area of need (Figure 2.2) may be found opposite.

The responsibilities of the subject teacher

You, as subject teacher, are responsible for the pupils with SEND in your classes. You hold responsibility for the learning and progress of pupils in your classes even where interventions involve group or one-to-one teaching or support *away* from the classroom. The questions below are designed to support debate among teachers about how this can be done effectively and manageably.

- Do you have opportunities for discussions with colleagues about how to improve teaching and provision for pupils with SEND?
- Do you feel you have the skills to plan to meet the needs of all pupils in your classes, including those with SEND?
- Is your school accessing evidence about 'what works' for pupils with SEND, such as the Sutton Trust Toolkit and the SpLD/Dyslexia Trust research?
- Are you able to access – and always able to understand the information in – reports written by other professionals?
- Do you have a plan for how you will be involved in monitoring the progress pupils are making as a result of SEN provision?
- How do you ensure that the skills being taught as part of SEN provision are practised and generalised in activities in your lessons?

Individual/Class/Group: Date/period:

Area of need	Provision	Pupil/s	Staff/pupil ratio	Cost per week	Outcomes/impact
Cognition and learning					
Communication and interaction					
Social, emotional and mental health difficulties					
Sensory and/or physical needs					

Figure 2.2 Template for provision map by area of need

- Are you confident that any additional adult support in your lessons is being used effectively and that it has a positive impact on the progress and development of pupils with SEND?
- How are you involved in measuring that impact?
- How do you ensure that pupils with SEND develop greater independence in your lessons?

Progression in curriculum content

It is important to ensure that as pupils move through the school they have access to new knowledge and experiences. The breadth of their learning experiences should not be limited by their SEND. A broadening curriculum as they progress through the school will extend pupils' knowledge and understanding, and prepare them for further education or employment. A developing awareness of personal, health, ethical and environmental issues will help pupils begin to make informed decisions about their own lives. For instance, an understanding of healthy eating may help a pupil make changes in his/her eating patterns, and so avoid potential health problems in later life. Teachers can support progression by planning opportunities for pupils to apply skills, knowledge and understanding in new contexts. Offering access to a variety of experiences, activities and environments appropriate to their chronological ages and interests helps pupils to generalise skills and understanding.

Progression in resources

Access over time to a differing range of resources in a school is an important part of progression. Pupils with SEND will become bored if they are expected always to work with primary books and equipment. Teachers might work together in faculty groups to identify a progression of resources across a subject. Consider the resources in your subject that pupils without SEND use as they move through the school, and identify ways in which the same or similar resources can be used or adapted to meet the needs of pupils with SEND. Above almost all else, avoid the pitfall of asking colleagues from primary schools to share their resources or workbooks. This might make your life easier but it will not help the pupil with SEND to make accelerated progress and could alienate him or her from other pupils.

Progression in teaching methods and support

As the pupil with SEND moves through the school, progression may be shown in the form of differing methods of teaching and support. Pupils need to begin to learn how to monitor and improve their own learning. Gradually, they should take responsibility for setting their own learning goals and can be supported to monitor their own progress against those goals. This progression towards greater independence is particularly important towards the end of Key Stage 3 as part of the preparation for transfer to further education or employment.

The style and level of support received by a pupil should be changed to show progression. A very 'hands-on' model of support may be appropriate in Key Stage 3, but in Key Stage 4 increasingly pupils should be expected to work independently. A gradual reduction in the level of adult support, and a greater expectation of co-operative work with other pupils, will support progression towards independence.

Problem solving

Everyone needs to develop the skills of problem solving, but pupils with SEND may rarely have opportunities to solve problems either individually or in groups. Pupils might be dependent on adult support and so reluctant to try new things by themselves, or sometimes it may be thought that they are not able to contribute to group activities which involve problem solving. Pupils with SEND must be encouraged to take risks and try new things. Sometimes they will make mistakes, but making mistakes and learning from them is a vital part of learning. To develop the skills of problem solving, start with individual or paired tasks based on real everyday activities. A visual or object framework in which to operate will give pupils the support they need.

Case study: Filipe

Filipe is a Year 9 pupil. The school is planning a Christmas fair and Filipe's class has been given the task of devising games for the families to play at the fair. Filipe and his friend Kieran decide to organise a 'Bat the Rat' game with support from two other boys and a learning mentor, Geoff. The boys watch a video of the game being played and George has made a list showing words and pictures of what they need to collect. With help from Geoff, the boys devise an action plan:

1   Using sugar paper, mock up a pipe to gauge how long it needs to be.
2   Buy a piece of drainpipe from the DIY store cut to the correct length.
3   Filipe to bring a toy mouse/rat from home (not forgetting to ask his sister's permission first).
4   Geoff to bring a wooden mallet from home.
5   Write out a rota for manning the game so that everyone has a chance to look around the fair.
6   Decide how much to charge for each go and who will be in charge of looking after the money.

The combination of visual support and supervision from Geoff and help from his friends meant that Filipe and Kieran were able successfully to do their bit for the Christmas fair. This kind of activity has a huge impact on the self-esteem of pupils with SEND, and enhances their role as part of the school community.

Setting small problems within other activities, where the pupil has to work something out to be able to continue, will help to begin the problem-solving process. For example, in a science lesson on electricity, the resources box contains everything the pupil needs to make a circuit except a battery. The pupil has a diagram that shows the battery. She looks in the neighbouring box and checks the contents. Realising what is missing, she asks the teacher for a battery. This small problem gave the pupil reasons to think, check, investigate, interact and communicate. Involving pupils who have SEND in group problem-solving activities will further develop these skills. In group activities such as maths trails using number, picture and written clues, other pupils will model thinking and problem-solving skills. Seeing and hearing how other people work things out is also an important part of the learning process.

Assessment beyond levels

As part of the reforms to the National Curriculum from September 2014, the previous system of 'levels' used to report pupils' attainment and progress was removed, and it will not be replaced. The intention behind this development is to allow teachers greater flexibility in the way that they plan and assess pupils' learning. The detailed specificity within core subjects provided by the revised national curriculum offers opportunities for assessments to be closely aligned to curriculum development and planning.

The removal of National Curriculum levels has led to schools working more collaboratively across areas and partnerships. This development gives teachers opportunities to become involved in, and have ownership over, planning assessment systems that allow pupils and parents to receive feedback that is more meaningful. The approaches that are then developed can be valuable to support teachers when they are planning differentiated approaches for personalised learning, and may enable pupils to have more active engagement in learning activities. This active engagement of all pupils will lead them, through enhanced self- and peer-assessment, to develop the skills to reflect on their learning.

Schools are free to develop their own systems of assessment, and to use a range of evaluation tools and evidence to evaluate whether pupils are making or exceeding the progress expected for their age and starting point. The challenge that schools face is that they must make sure assessments are meaningful and accurate, not only in the context of their own school, but also in the context of other local schools. A school may develop an assessment system that works well for itself, but that has no relevance to the systems in use in the local feeder primary schools or FE colleges to which pupils transfer. Whatever system your school adopts or develops, it must be sufficiently robust to allow for both internal and external moderation and scrutiny. 'Inspectors must assure themselves that the methods used are robust and that the school's attainment data are accurate and reliable' (*School Inspection Handbook*, Ofsted, 2014, p. 69). Assessment of progress and attainment for pupils with SEND will need to be considered in a broader sense than merely that of academic achievement. A range of tools should be employed to gain a full perspective of a child's strengths and needs. This range could include:

- Classroom observation schedules completed by teachers and teaching assistants.
- Book trawl/work scrutiny.
- Self-assessment and recording tools for pupils, using approaches such as success criteria checklists, 'I can' statements, and 'two stars and a wish'.
- Questionnaires, for pupils and for parents.
- Early Support School Age Developmental Journal.
- Standardised tests.
- Screening schedules and profiling tools such as those for behaviour or SLCN.

- Regular assessments, such as reading records.
- Key objectives checklists.
- School tracking systems.
- Diagnostic assessments carried out by specialists, such as speech and language therapists, or educational psychologists.

Assessment for learning and teaching

The 'Assessment for Learning' (AfL) approach originated as a response to the need for assessment to be more consistent with current approaches to teaching and learning. The first priority of the AfL approach is to promote pupils' learning, rather than mere account-ability. AfL activities provide information to be used as feedback by teachers, and for their pupils in assessing themselves and each other. This facility modifies the teaching and learning activities in which they are engaged (Black *et al.*, 2004, p. 10). Although AfL developed as an approach for all pupils, it is particularly relevant for children and young people with SEND as it underpins good quality teaching and supports 'meta-learning' – pupils thinking and talking about learning and developing an understanding of *how* they learn.

Assessment for Learning:

- is part of effective planning;
- is central to classroom practice;
- promotes understanding of goals and criteria;
- is sensitive and constructive;
- fosters motivation;
- recognises all educational achievement;
- focuses on how pupils learn;
- helps learners know how to improve;
- develops the capacity for peer and self-assessment;
- is a key professional skill.

(*Assessment for Learning: Effects and Impact*, María Teresa Flórez and Pamela Sammons, Oxford University, Department of Education, CfBT Education Trust, 2013, pp. 3–4)

The P scales in mainstream secondary schools

The P scales originally were designed to facilitate whole-school target-setting for special schools. They remain a useful assessment tool for tracking the attainment of individuals and of groups of pupils, and provide a common vocabulary for assessing pupils in all settings, including mainstream secondary schools.

The P scales were an important and powerful development. Important because they were the first attempt to link the attainments of pupils with more significant learning difficulties directly to the National Curriculum levels of attainment, and powerful because they can support mainstream schools in meeting and assessing the needs of pupils with learning difficulties. The P scales offer mainstream schools tools to inform appropriate and achievable targets for pupils with more significant learning difficulties, and to record small steps of progress. They provide a framework of common performance measures, and support the detailed assessment of pupil attainment for reports and review meetings.

The challenge for the future is that currently there is no national, statutory, moderation of P scales, and the guidance materials are out of date. It will be up to secondary schools to work together with their feeder mainstream primaries and special schools to develop local moderation protocols that are robust and meaningful across all contexts.

Progression for pupils with complex SEND

For pupils with complex SEND, progression needs to be planned in terms of experiences, resources and contexts, as well as by means of more traditional academic progress. Some pupils with complex SEND will access the curriculum mainly through their senses and need activities that involve active exploration:

- feeling different textures;
- experiencing different kinds of movement;
- tasting a range of foods;
- smelling perfumes, herbs and flowers;
- listening to music and environmental sounds;
- looking at, and through, colours and visual effects.

Linking these sensory activities to age-appropriate subject contexts will ensure progression. To give these experiences in isolation creates a stagnant situation that is not stimulating either for the child or for those adults working with the child.

Case study: Bonita

Bonita is in Year 7 and has complex SEND. She communicates using eye-gaze and facial expression. One of her learning targets is to maintain her head in an upright position. For part of each day Bonita works with her teaching assistant in a sensory area created from a large cupboard. One afternoon her teaching assistant was called away urgently, and no one was available to cover for her, so Bonita joined in the art lesson with her peer group. Several pupils supported her over the course of the lesson and she smiled throughout as she made hand-prints on paper. The art teacher noticed that Bonita had held her head up throughout the lesson and she was much more alert than in the one-to-one situation in the sensory room.

With a little thought and creativity, activities can be built into whole-class lessons in secondary schools. Below is an example of a pupil with complex SEND included in a Year 9 music lesson.

Case study: Pardeep

Pardeep is in Year 9. He uses a wheelchair for all his time in school. He has always attended mainstream school and especially loves the company of the boys in his class. Pardeep communicates by eye pointing and smiling.

Pardeep's learning targets for music are:

- to communicate consistent preferences by eye pointing; and
- to link music/sounds with objects.

Background

Pardeep accesses the curriculum through all his senses. While listening is the primary sense used here, the teacher has collected a number of objects that Pardeep looks at and holds to link to the short extracts of music that he hears. The other pupils in the class are working on the composition of short pieces of music using a range of instruments.

As each extract of music is played, the appropriate object is passed to Pardeep. The objects have been chosen because of their differing shapes and textures.

Over a number of weeks Pardeep develops the ability to look at the correct object when the associated track is played and also can choose the order of objects, again using eye pointing, so creating his own piece of music. Pardeep joins the rest of the class to listen to all their compositions, including his own. Pardeep's responses throughout the lessons are recorded on camera and video. This evidence of his experiences and progress is stored in the Experience Folder on his wiki.

Physical, orientation and mobility skills

Pupils with complex SEND will have additional priorities of physical, orientation and mobility skills that have to be addressed in school. These skills include:

- fine motor skills, such as grasping, holding and manipulating;
- whole body skills, such as the co-ordination of movement, rolling and walking;
- positioning skills, such as head control;
- tolerating and/or managing mobility aids, such as a wheelchair, walking frame or splints.

These priorities can usually be addressed in mainstream classes without recourse to specialist equipment.

Fine motor skills can be developed in:

- art and design – working with a range of media and textures;
- design and technology – joining components;
- music – exploring and playing percussion instruments;
- maths – creating different sizes of sets of objects.

Whole body skills can be developed in:

- drama – exploring different kinds of movement;
- PE and games – lying and sitting on the trampoline, gymnastics;
- dance – exploring body shapes, moving in time to music.

Positioning skills, and tolerating and managing mobility aids, can be developed in all lessons and other school situations. Practising these priorities in the supported setting of a school will prepare pupils for the move to further education and for living in their local community.

Pupils with additional medical priorities

For those pupils who have significant medical needs in addition to complex SEND, the concept of progress may be more difficult to define. The progress of pupils with degenerative diseases may need to be defined in terms of maintaining, rather than extending, skills and understanding. Progress and progression can be defined in terms of the breadth of the experiences in which the pupil is involved.

The Education, Health and Care assessment and planning process

Across England, up to 20 per cent of children and young people are identified as having special educational needs and disabilities, but only about 2 per cent will need EHC plans. This means that the majority of children and young people with SEND will have all their learning needs met successfully in their local mainstream school without the need for an education, health and care needs assessment or plan.

The move to EHC plans is designed to create an assessment and planning process that is holistic, co-ordinated, and most importantly centred around the views, interests and aspirations of the child or young person and his or her family. This family-centred process is sometimes called 'person-centred', in that the pupil and his or her family are at the heart of the process and are closely involved in all decisions made about provision and interventions. Indeed, the final EHC plan should be a co-produced document, meaning that the pupil, his or her parents, and professionals, work together as equals to produce a tailored plan personalised to the needs and aspirations of the pupil and his or her family.

The EHC process brings together the support and provision from education, health, and social care services that enable the pupil to achieve the best possible educational and other outcomes. The EHC assessment and planning process is underpinned by a requirement on local authorities and Clinical Commissioning Groups (CCGs) jointly to commission services for children and young people with SEND.

Education, Health and Care needs assessment

The EHC needs assessment is the first stage in the process and the criteria or threshold for a needs assessment is relatively low – that the child or young person has special educational needs and that it *may* be necessary for him or her to have an EHC plan – not that it probably *will* be necessary, just that it is a real possibility.

When making the decision whether or not to go ahead with an EHC needs assessment, a local authority will consider a range of evidence, including evidence from school.

Local authorities always ask schools for advice and information about the pupil when they are considering whether or not to issue an EHC plan, so it is important that you, as one of a team of teachers working with the pupil, have the necessary evidence available before the school requests an EHC needs assessment for a pupil, or as soon as a parent lets you know that they have made a request themselves.

The information that school will need to have to hand includes:

- records of regular SEN reviews with parents and the pupil;
- any learning plans and targets;
- records of attainment and progress;
- the nature and extent of the pupil's SEN;
- evidence of the action by school to meet the pupil's SEN;
- evidence of the progress that has been made as a result of the additional and different special educational provision in school;
- evidence of the pupil's physical, emotional and social development.

Who can request an EHC needs assessment?

The people who have a specific right to ask a local authority to carry out an EHC needs assessment for a pupil are:

- the child or young person's parent;
- a person acting on behalf of the school;
- anyone else who thinks an EHC needs assessment may be necessary. This could include foster carers, health and social care professionals, or a family friend.

Where schools make the request, this should be with the knowledge, and wherever possible the agreements, of the pupil's parents. Whoever makes the request, the local authority will always inform the parents to let them know they are considering the request and to ascertain the parents' views. At this early stage, local authorities will follow the Section 19 principles, and pay particular attention to the views, wishes and feelings of the child or young person and his or her parent, and establish how they can best be kept informed and supported to participate as fully as possible in the decision making.

What is expected progress?

In deciding whether an EHC needs assessment is required, local authorities consider whether there is evidence that, despite the school having taken relevant and purposeful action to identify, assess and meet the special educational needs of the child or young person, the child or young person has not made expected progress (SEND Code of Practice, 2015, 9.14, p. 145).

All pupils do not make, and are not expected to make, the same progress. For example, a pupil with Down's syndrome may be making very good progress, but that progress might still be slower than that of other pupils in his/her year group. When you are deciding whether or not to put forward a request for an EHC needs assessment, you and the pupil's parents need to consider whether he or she is making expected progress – that is, progress that is:

- similar to the progress of the pupil's peers starting from the same baseline;
- matches or is better than the pupil's previous rate of progress; or
- closes the attainment gap between the pupil and other pupils in the same year group.

It is worth remembering that an EHC needs assessment will not always lead to an EHC plan, and schools will need to help parents understand this. Even if following the needs assessment the local authority decides not to issue a plan, the information that is collected during the assessment will be made available to the school to inform and improve the SEN provision for the individual pupil.

Education, Health and Care plans

The purpose of an Education, Health and Care (EHC) plan is:

- to make special educational provision to meet the special educational needs of the child or young person;
- to secure the best possible outcomes for the pupil across education, health and social care and, as they get older,
- to prepare him or her for adulthood.

EHC plans should be forward-looking documents that outline the provision required to support the pupil in achieving his or her ambitions. They should specify how services will be delivered as part of a whole package, and explain how best to achieve across education, health and social care, the outcomes sought for the child.

Within all EHC plans there are a number of mandatory sections. All EHC plans include Sections A to K, but there is no requirement for these sections to be in alphabetical order. Each local authority has its own template for the EHC plan that includes a range of different elements. Most plan templates include a section for information about the family's strengths and needs – sometimes called 'My story'. Others use a one-page profile template (see Figure 1.2) to capture this information and to outline what is important to the child and his or her family and the best ways to support them.

The mandatory sections of the EHC plan are:

A   The views, interests and aspirations of the child for the future.
B   The child's special educational needs.
C   The child's health needs.
D   The child's social care needs.
E   The outcomes for the next two or three years or phase of education.
F   The special educational provision needed to help the child to achieve his or her outcomes.
G   Any health provision reasonably required.
H1 & H2   Social care provision.
I   Name and type of school.
J   Personal budget.
K   Advice and information gathered.

Most pupils who are issued with an EHC plan will continue to attend and have all their special needs met at the local mainstream school – only a small minority will need a placement in a special school or other specialist provision. The EHC needs assessment will provide the school with a wealth of information on which to base the provision for the individual child, but should also prompt the school, and especially the pupil's subject teachers, to review the entirety of the educational provision for that pupil and for all the pupils. For example, an EHC plan might include physiotherapy to improve a pupil's mobility. It is likely that in addition to working with the individual pupil, the physio-therapist will give advice to the school on how to support the pupil in all lessons, such as with the correct type and size of chair and positioning. This information can then be used to support improvements in seating arrangements for other pupils in the school. The following is an example.

A visiting mentor supporting a student teacher noticed that while a number of the pupils in a Year 8 lesson could not put their feet on the floor because the chairs were too big, others could not fit their knees under the tables because the chairs were too small. The furniture simply did not accommodate the wide range of heights in the class. The mentor mentioned this observation to an assistant headteacher who consulted the physiotherapist for advice. A range of chairs in differing sizes and colours were then made available and students were able to choose a chair appropriate for them. This led to noticeable improvements in pupils' concentration, behaviour and progress.

Even when a pupil has an EHC plan, the graduated approach cycle of assess, plan, do and review will continue alongside regular reviews of progress with parents.

Summary

The introduction of SEN Support and the EHC process requires everyone involved to adopt person-centred approaches. This means new demands on schools; demands especially upon a closer working relationship with families of children with SEND. Those schools that have already started on this path have found that co-operation and co-production with families is hugely beneficial in improving outcomes for all. This emphasis on the raising of aspirations and achieving the best possible educational and other outcomes for children with SEND is a call to arms for all of us who care so passionately about these children. As Michelangelo said: 'The greatest danger is not that our aim is too high and we miss it, but that our aim is too low and we hit it.'

Chapter 3

Working with families
Section 19 in action

Section 19 of the Children and Families Act 2014 sets out the core principles of the legislation. The principles are that local authorities must pay particular attention to:

- The views, wishes and feelings of children and their parents, and young people.
- The importance of them participating as fully as possible in decision making and the provision of information and support to enable them to do so.
- Supporting children and young people's development and helping them to achieve the best possible educational and other outcomes.

(Children and Families Act, 2014, Section 19)

This chapter focuses on the first two of these principles within the context of the secondary school. Recent research shows that by addressing the first two principles pupils are more likely to achieve the best possible educational and other outcomes. Working with families is not an optional extra to school improvement; it is a well-evidenced route to improved attainment and progress.

What does the research tell us?

In their review of best practice in parental engagement Goodall and Vorhaus (2011) cited the work of Greenough *et al.* (2007)'s research that examined how progress in children's attainment and their dispositions to learn can be supported through knowledge-exchange activities between school and home, and home and school. The research showed that following these knowledge-exchange activities students appeared to adjust more quickly to secondary school than students in the comparison group (Greenhough *et al.*, 2007; see also Harris and Goodall, 2009).

Schools often perceive parents as 'hard to reach' (Crozier and Davies, 2007 and Sherbert Research, 2009) or uninterested (De Gaetano, 2007) and do not always respond to or acknowledge the efforts parents are already making with their children (De Fraja, 2010). Whereas, on the other hand, parents often consider that their interactions with their children are either undervalued by schools, or have little value in themselves. High levels of educational expectations, consistent encouragement and actions that enhance the learning opportunities of children are the family practices that are associated with positive educational experiences. Importantly, the relationships between parental involvement and educational outcomes exist regardless of students' socioeconomic or race/ethnic background (Catsambis, 2001).

It is clear from research over a number of years that parental engagement is a powerful lever for raising student achievement in schools. Where parents and teachers work together to improve learning, the gains in achievement are significant. Rather than support activities in the school, parents have the greatest influence on the achievement of their children through supporting their learning in the home. It is their support of learning within the home environment that makes the maximum difference to achievement (Harris and Goodall, 2007).

A major challenge to successful parental engagement is often the reluctance of teachers to work with parents as equal partners. To engage effectively with parents, teachers and other school staff need to have training and ongoing coaching to give them opportunities for reflection and feedback. This training is especially important when teachers are working with parents whose backgrounds and cultures may be very different from their own. Training for teachers was a key feature of the Achievement for All pilot project in 2009 to 2011, and in the evaluation report (Humphreys and Squires, 2011) the structured conversations with parents were shown to be the most successful aspect of the project in terms of both pupil outcomes and parental engagement (p. 8).

Planning for parent engagement

Despite all the evidence, very few schools set aside part of their budgets to support parental engagement. There is a cost to engaging parents – the cost of releasing teachers to have meaningful conversations with families and to make home visits; for the making of a welcoming and comfortable place in the school for parents to meet and learn together; for resources and workshops to help parents support their children's learning at home. Without this funding teachers feel under pressure to finish meetings quickly so as to get back to class, and parents will continue to feel distanced from their child's learning. To develop real and meaningful parent engagement, schools must take the initiative in their collaboration with families. School leaders should share their belief that the engagement of all parents is of paramount importance to staff members across all levels.

Collaboration with parents that is sensitive to the whole range of family circumstances and tailored to local contexts and circumstances is a strong and effective driver of school improvement. The Achievement for All pilot programme showed that the successful collaborative relationships that were formed between teachers and parents involved a two-way exchange of information, ideas, aspirations and concerns, and that the schools valued the contributions that parents had to make to their child's education and to the whole educational process. The following is an example.

A secondary school introduced termly conversations with parents of pupils with SEND in Years 9 and 10 in a pilot project to improve GCSE results for those pupils. In one conversation the 'difficult and demanding' parents of a pupil in Year 10 shared with their key teacher the story of the traumatic pregnancy, delivery and neonatal period of their son's life. It was clear that the parents still felt very emotional about this period and that, as a result, they continued to be very protective of their son. This information helped the key teacher to gain a better understanding of both the pupil and his family, and his sensitive facilitation of the conversation led to a much better relationship between the family and school, and to improved progress for the pupil. As one headteacher said, 'Parents are rarely hard to reach . . . they're just scared to come in.'

Another key feature of schools that have effective and sustainable parental engagement is that the actions taken to develop that engagement were based on a sound knowledge of their local community, and of the families of the pupils in the school. The key actions in the planning cycle for these schools were:

- *A needs analysis*: the schools carried out comprehensive needs analyses so that they knew which parents were engaged, and identified the barriers to engagement and involvement faced by families, such as work commitments, younger children, transport, and language.
- *Mutual priorities*: the schools worked with families to agree priorities for their individual children and for the whole school.
- *A whole-school evaluation of resources*: the schools allocated budgets to support the engagement of parents.
- *A strategic plan*: co-produced with parents which identified the necessary adjustments to systems and organisation.
- *An awareness-raising process* which helped parents and teachers understand and commit to the strategic plan.

(Goodall and Vorhaus, 2011, p. 85)

Parent engagement doesn't just happen. It must be planned for and embedded in a whole-school strategy.

A parental engagement strategy should be the subject of ongoing support, monitoring, and development. This will include strategic planning which embeds parental engagement in whole-school development plans, sustained support, resourcing and training, community involvement at all levels of management, and a continuous system of evidence based development and review.

(Goodall and Vorhaus, 2011, p. 10)

When a pupil has special educational needs or a disability, it is not only that child or young person who is affected. All the family to a greater or lesser extent will feel the impact of the child's additional needs – parents, brothers and sisters, grandparents, even uncles, aunts and cousins. By the time their child starts secondary school, the family has had eleven years of anxiety, challenges and, in many cases, grief. Each family will respond to and cope with those experiences in different ways: some will be very angry, while others may appear less concerned and get on with the job of raising their child, but that anxiety will still be there.

Adding to the pressures and anxiety of having a child with SEND, parents and families also have to deal with a deluge of advice and information from professionals. They are required to attend frequent appointments, which sometimes involve long journeys. All these professionals are busy people, and parents often are reluctant to ask questions or seek clarification because they do not wish to take up valuable time. This can lead to misunderstandings, and to even more anxiety.

By the time the child reaches secondary-school age parents may be wary of yet another tranche of education professionals. Each of these professionals will have their own area of expertise and have a different slant on the child's strengths and needs. Parents can feel that their voice is the least important, and may begin to lose confidence in their own ability to raise their son or daughter. As discussed in the previous chapter, the Children and Families Act (2014) and the resulting SEND Code of Practice (2015) raise the expectations on all professionals from education, health and social care, as to how they work with the parents of children and young people with SEND.

Case study: Jacob

Jacob is a much wanted second son. His mum had a normal pregnancy and delivery, and Jacob was an 'easy' baby for the first six weeks, rarely crying and seemingly content. Jacob sat at one year and walked at eighteen months. He was reluctant to eat solids and, when finally weaned, would eat only a limited range of foods, and although he showed affection towards his parents, he did not bring things to show them or point to interesting objects – he didn't share attention. At two years old, Jacob was diagnosed as having Autistic Spectrum Disorder (ASD). His family read all they could about ASD and in time they realised how severely affected he was by the condition. Jacob is a much-loved son, but his family still feel the loss of the child they hoped he might have become.

The Lamb Inquiry

The Lamb Inquiry (2009) into special educational needs and parental confidence found evidence of 'an underlying culture where parents and carers of children with SEN can be seen as the problem resulting in parent carers losing confidence in schools and professionals'. The findings of the Lamb Inquiry have had a profound influence on the Children and Families Act 2014 and the SEND Code of Practice. This should lead to a significant change in both the culture and practice of settings, schools, colleges and other professionals in their work with and for the parent carers of children and young people with SEND.

Supporting families through transition

The move from primary to secondary school can be just as daunting for the family as it is for the child. Primary schools generally provide a smaller and supportive environment for children and parents alike. Some parents will need care and guidance to help them understand and be comfortable with the different expectations and routines of secondary school.

Invite parents to spend some time in the school before the child transfers, and go through the necessary documentation with them such as the school prospectus, or the key points of the SEN Information Report. For parents who experience difficulties with literacy, have this vital information available in different formats, including as an audio file. Information in other languages or access to an interpreter is necessary where English is not the home language, or in other formats should parents or other family members have a visual or hearing impairment.

The SEND Code of Practice 2015 emphasises the importance of schools gathering information, including holding an early discussion with the pupil and their parents, not only to give information, but also to draw on the parents' knowledge and concerns about their child. This early discussion is also an opportunity to tell parents about the local authority's information, advice and support service, and other local parent-carers organisations (SEND Code of Practice, 2015, 6.39, p. 99).

Parents usually are delighted that their child has the opportunity to be educated alongside friends from primary school, but they will also have an additional anxiety as to how their child will manage in a mainstream secondary school. Families' concerns are often not only about their own child, but also about other children:

'How will they react to having a pupil with SEND in their classes?'

'Will other pupils' work be disrupted?'

'Will the additional work for the teachers mean less time for the rest of the class?'

Parents may even be in conflict with other family members or friends over the decision to send their child to mainstream secondary school. Though inclusion is no longer a new concept, grandparents and older family members may expect a child with more significant and complex needs to be 'cared for' in a special school. These concerns can be assuaged if teachers and teaching assistants maintain an open and positive dialogue with parents and reassure the family that the child is a valued member of the school.

It is important to recognise the individuality of families and the uniqueness of each pupil. Schools need to be flexible, respectful and non-judgemental in their dealings with families, whatever form a family may take. A starting point is to listen to parent carers and make sure that their opinions are respected and valued as much as, or more than, those of professionals.

Parents as partners

As part of their mission statement, schools often state that they work in 'partnership with parents'. Both for parents and for schools, what does that mean in practice? With parents in general and parents of pupils with SEND in particular, schools need to develop a culture not only of co-operation but also of collaboration and co-production, requiring a much deeper level of partnership. In order for partnership to have any meaning, schools have to value parents' views, experience and expertise, and use parents' skills to complement and build upon what happens in the classroom. To acknowledge the parents' role as their child's prime educators is the first step in establishing a true partnership. The work of schools is more effective when parents are involved, and where account is taken of their feelings and unique perspectives. In practice, this will mean:

- full parental involvement in planning the transition from primary into secondary school;
- parents empowered and supported to take an active role in their child's education;
- parents helped to recognise and fulfil their responsibilities as well as knowing their rights;
- schools listening and giving a positive response to parents' views;
- parents given access to appropriate and timely information, advice and support, especially during assessments;

- sharing all information about a pupil with his or her parents in 'user-friendly' ways and language;
- the development of family-friendly procedures designed to engage and include all parents;
- sharing and acknowledging how parents and school staff feel about the pupil, and his or her place in the school. For example:

> 'I am anxious about meeting his needs' (teacher).
> 'We are hurt when other parents complain about our child' (parents).
> 'Seeing him make progress has been a real delight for me' (teaching assistant).

True partnership comes about through mutual respect and positive attitudes. Schools may need to offer additional support and encouragement to families of pupils with SEND – to go 'the extra mile' to make the partnership work. It will be worth it.

Advice and guidance for parents

Some parents will be unsure about how secondary schools operate, and the expectations that teachers will have of them and their child. They may base their expectations on their own experiences of secondary school, not all of which will be positive. They will need to be guided through the network of requirements and responsibilities that go along with the education of a pupil with special educational needs or disability.

A great deal of information will be given to parents when they visit the school for the first time, or at an open afternoon or evening. An additional and individual appointment with the form tutor, head of year, or SENCO, will encourage the parents of a pupil with SEND to ask questions more pertinent to their own child. This less formal situation will begin to develop trust between parents and school.

Some parents may find it helpful to involve a third party such as a family member, or an adviser from the SEND Information, Advice and Support Service (SENDIASS), or another parent from a local support group. This 'outside' person may act as a supporter for parents, and can mediate between home and school when parents are anxious or unsure. However, this liaison should not get in the way of direct communication and co-operation.

Resolving disputes

Misunderstandings or disputes about provision or progress are less likely to occur where schools work closely with parents as a pupil settles into the school. It is when parents feel sidelined or patronised that problems start to build up, and it is then very difficult to regain lost confidence and trust.

When a disagreement does occur, teachers at all costs should avoid a situation deteriorating into communication only by increasingly acrimonious letters, or into a full breakdown in communication. Defuse the situation with a home visit, or at the very least a telephone call to discuss a way forward, even if you then agree to disagree. Disputes are like a virus that can poison all areas of the relationship between school and home. In the long run the pupil and his or her parents will still be a part of the school, and it is important that they are helped once again to feel part of that community.

Parental priorities: the long view

Secondary schools educate and care for children for up to seven years, which is a long time, but only a small proportion of a child's whole life. Parents have a constant and continuing responsibility, and have to take a much longer view into the future, even beyond a time when they themselves will be able to care for their son or daughter. This latter concern is ever-present for families of children with SEN or disabilities who would not wish siblings to have to take on the responsibility for their brother or sister. Because of this concern parents are likely to have additional and sometimes different priorities and aspirations from those of a school, and often linked to life and independent 'survival' skills.

These priorities might be:

- *basic skills*: reading, writing and numeracy, so that their child will be able to sign their name, understand and fill in a form, or check their change in a shop;
- *communication*: being able to hold a conversation or ask for help;
- *self-help skills*: being able to care for themselves, including their personal hygiene;
- *domestic skills*: being able to cook a simple meal or keep a home clean;
- *community or social skills*: being able to behave appropriately in a café, supermarket or youth club;
- *independence*: being able to use public transport and access leisure facilities;
- *relationships*: having their own friends and a full social life;
- *safety*: from exploitation, violence or abuse.

In the secondary phase of education, many of these priorities will be addressed through the wider curriculum. Other priorities will be covered as part of the parents' role in the day-to-day course of family life. When teachers talk about learning targets in SEN review meetings, parents will want to know how those targets impact on their own aspirations for their child. It is all very well Reena having a target to 'start tasks quickly and maintain focus during completion', but her parents need to be helped to understand just *how* such a target as this will help their child become independent in the future.

Dreams and aspirations activity

This is a valuable and practical activity that links the views, priorities and aspirations of the pupil and his or her family to medium-term and short-term learning targets. It can be used as a part of the initial Education, Health and Care planning process or for annual reviews of EHC plans.

1   Invite parents and other family members either to come into school or, if the family is reluctant to come to school, to a neutral venue, such as a village hall. Allow at least an hour for the meeting, and include the child and his or her form tutor. If the activity is part of the EHC planning process or annual review, professionals from health and, where appropriate, social care, can be invited. The parents, form tutor or SENCO should act as facilitator.
2   Prepare the room in advance. Around the walls stick five or six sheets of flipchart paper.

3   The facilitator welcomes everyone to the meeting and explains the activity. The key principle is that no one's opinion is more important than another's – everyone has an equal voice – and that the purpose of the activity is to 'co-produce' a plan for the pupil together.

4   Start the activity by asking the pupil, his or her parents, and any other family members to go to one of the sheets of flipchart paper. Ask the pupil to draw or write what they want for themselves when they become an adult. It doesn't matter if the dreams seem far-fetched or unattainable; even if a pupil says he wants to be an astronaut, it will be a clue to his motivations and interests, and can be used as a context for learning and motivation. Next, ask the family to think about and write or draw what their dreams are for the child or young person when he or she is an adult.

5   When the family has finished, explain that the dreams and aspirations that they have captured will be used as starting points for planning outcomes for the next two or three years or phase of education. Display this first sheet of paper at one end of the room.

6   Move to the next sheet of paper and at the top write 'Outcomes'. Again, ask the pupil first and then his or her family and any professionals present what they want him or her to achieve in the next two or three years. What outcomes does the pupil need to achieve in this time scale if he or she is to have any chance of achieving the aspirations on the first flipchart paper?

7   Move to the next (third) sheet of paper and at the top write 'this year'. Still focusing on the long-term aspirations but also having in mind the outcomes, what will the pupil need to achieve over the next year if he or she is to achieve those outcomes? Also into the equation at this point comes the head of year or SENCO's and teachers' knowledge of national expectations of progress for all pupils, including those with SEND.

8   The final stage of the process is for the pupil, the parents and the teacher to commit to what each of them will do to help the child or young person achieve their outcomes. These commitments are a vital element of the process and should be recorded against each of the outcomes.

Open and relaxed dialogue between school and parents will ensure that parental priorities and aspirations can be incorporated into education planning at times appropriate to the pupil's development. If this planning does not take place duplication of effort will occur, leading to a waste of valuable time.

Case study: Jemma

Jemma is in Year 10. She joins the GCSE art class for a double period each week. Jemma has cerebral palsy and complex learning difficulties. She uses her wheelchair in school, and spends part of each day in a standing frame. Jemma is supported by a teaching assistant, Fatima, when in school. One of Jemma's targets is to show curiosity and to investigate her environment. Fatima spends half an hour each day one-to-one with Jemma on this target, using a range of objects and sounds. When the Year 10 group was working on the relationship between three-dimensional design and urban, rural and other settings, the pupils collected a variety of materials from both the rural and urban environments. Jemma explored these materials without prompts and showed real interest in the differing textures and colours. When the other pupils worked on their structures, they created harsh lighting and listened to loud music. The air was full of the odours of welding and melting plastic. They were surrounded by the sounds of metal being beaten and bent. Jemma found these lessons totally stimulating, looking around constantly and vocalizing to show her pleasure in the experience. These art lessons did much more to help Jemma make progress against her targets than daily more sterile one-to-one exercises.

Communicating with parents and other family members

Communication with the parents of pupils with SEND is a crucial element in his or her education and wider development, but one that can easily go wrong. This is especially possible where pupils are transported to school by taxi or minibus, and where the requirement and opportunity for parents to visit the school are less frequent. This situation makes other forms of communication between home and school even more important. Here are some ideas for moving beyond home-school diaries into other more creative and direct ways to maintain close links with families.

Email and text messages

Emails and texts are excellent ways to develop and maintain communication between home and school. A general message can be sent out to all parents daily or weekly, with individual messages and photographs added where needed. Copies of schemes of work or lesson plans can be shared in this way so that parents can reinforce the concepts that have been taught and support any resulting homework. Emails and texts are more informal, and may be less threatening to some parents. Replying to electronic messages is also quick and easy and will encourage busy parents to respond – and an email can't be eaten by next-door's dog!

School calendars and diaries

School calendars or diaries are a useful and unobtrusive method of communicating with parents. A written comment or a sticky note attached to the page for the day gives the necessary information simply and discreetly. There is also an added benefit of including important dates to remind school, parents and pupil about hospital appointments, when items such as sports kits or musical instruments need to be brought to school, or when homework is due to be given in.

Phone calls

Some parents need an even more personal approach. When a pupil has worked well, tried hard, or achieved a personal goal, a telephone call to the parents will be really appreciated.

Build up direct positive contacts – this is a way of developing trust between school and parents, and will make future problems easier to resolve. A phone call often sorts out minor misunderstandings and is especially helpful to parents who may themselves have problems with reading and numeracy. A couple of timely calls may avoid a great deal of paperwork and ill feeling.

Home visits

Home visits are not usually an aspect of secondary school practice, but they are the most effective way of developing positive communication with parents of pupils with SEND. The head of year, the SENCO, or form tutor are the ideal people to make the home visits as they can then feed back the information to subject teachers and support staff. The visits should begin before the pupil starts at the school, and ideally should be repeated a couple of times over the course of Year 7, and if necessary, for longer. This contact with parents will give the background to the child or young person's learning and behaviour. The understanding gained informs learning targets and objectives, and makes planning for learning more specific to the pupil's needs.

Meet the pupil in the home context and this will have other benefits. Pupils are much more likely to be confident, happy, and well behaved in classes when they know their teachers and parents know each other well, are in regular communication, and are working together.

Sharing information

An open communication with parents especially brings other benefits when sharing information about the child. The more information a school has about the pupil the better able it will be to meet a child's particular educational and social needs.

Difficulties at home

Family crises are, of course, private matters, but schools need to be informed that the pupil may be experiencing anxiety or distress, even if the details are kept confidential. Should a pupil's behaviour or mood in school change significantly, and before putting into place any behaviour plan, always contact parents first. The changes may not be linked to the child or young person's SEND, but could reflect a problem at home. Something as minor as mum being in bed with the flu for a few days can cause huge anxiety for a pupil with SEND, and where a pupil has limited or impaired communication skills, behaviour may be his/her only way of expressing distress.

Medical information

It is especially important for a school to have certain medical information when including pupils with SEND. Any information will have to come from parents, and must be treated confidentially and with sensitivity. Once parents have shared this information the school can seek out any training necessary, and put systems in place for administering medication. Where pupils receive all their medication at home, parents may not appreciate the importance of telling school about prescription changes, and changes in medication may have profound effects on concentration, learning and behaviour.

Case study: Kelly

Kelly is in Year 9 of her local secondary school. She has a significant developmental delay and additional health and attention difficulties. Kelly's behaviour in school had improved dramatically over the previous term, but she also appeared lethargic much of the time and lunchtime supervisors noticed that she had lost her appetite. Kelly's form tutor rang her mum to ask if these changes were apparent at home, or if mum knew of a reason why Kelly's demeanour should have altered. Mum told the teacher that Kelly's medication had been changed following an appointment with the consultant. Mum had not realised that she would need to inform the school about the medication change, assuming that information of this kind would routinely be shared between professionals.

When a teacher notices a marked change in the behaviour or mood of a pupil with SEND, it is always worth checking with parents to see whether there has been any change at home in circumstances or medication. A quick phone call will save a great deal of time in the long run.

Parents must feel confident that the school will provide effective support for their child's medical condition, and that their child will be safe in school. Local healthcare services and professionals are often very willing to offer advice to schools, but most important is that schools listen to and value the views, expertise and knowledge of parents and pupils.

Absences

Because of hospital or therapy appointments or visits to specialist centres – such as for conductive education or assessment for communication aids – pupils with SEND may have more absences from school than other students. Inevitably, these absences will have an effect on the pupil's learning and progress. Wherever possible, consultations, assessments or therapy should take place in school. Many professionals welcome coming into school, as this arrangement offers them the chance to observe the pupil in the natural classroom setting, and to speak to the teachers and teaching assistants working with the pupil.

Where absences cannot be avoided – for instance, because of illness or important hospital appointments, teachers can keep in touch with the family by phone or email. This will help the parents and the pupil feel they remain an important part of the school community. Sending home a short note, or a couple of books or a game, lets parents know how much the school cares about them and their child, and reinforces the value of learning.

Links with parents' organisations and charities

Charities and parents' organisations such as the National Autistic Society, the Communication Trust, the Dyslexia SpLD Trust, and the Down's Syndrome Association, are valuable sources of information and advice for schools. They produce excellent materials for schools on facilitating access to the curriculum and on the management of medical issues. These organisations can also support schools more directly, such as advising on inclusive extra-curricular activities in which all pupils can participate, or delivering a series of workshops for parents, or assemblies for groups of pupils, all of which increases awareness and understanding of particular disabilities among other parents and pupils.

Shared training

To meet the needs of a particular pupil schools need to arrange training on issues specific to that child or young person. This training will be more effective if parents are included or, even better, asked to be part of the training team. In this way 'everyone knows what everyone knows', and parents are given an equal status alongside professionals. Parents are the prime care-giver and they really do know their child better than anyone else; their knowledge and expertise should be harnessed by the school as a vital resource.

Training to be shared with, or led by, parents

Health or therapy issues linked to particular disabilities or syndromes

For example:

- Help for a pupil who has breathing difficulties.
- Mobility exercises for a pupil with cerebral palsy.
- Developing an occupational therapy programme in school, etc.

Classroom strategies to support a pupil with a learning difficulty or a sensory impairment

For example:

- Positioning in class to maximise hearing or vision.
- Structured teaching.
- Support to enable the pupil to manage his own hearing aids.
- The use of IT to support a pupil with a visual impairment, etc.

The administration of medication

For example:

- Epilepsy medication;
- insulin injections;
- use of inhalers or nebulisers.

Shared training is a valuable route to greater understanding and co-operation between parents and school staff. It gives parents, teachers and teaching assistants time to focus on the pupil in a positive way and to develop the trust necessary for an effective partnership.

Short breaks

Despite being very important to parents, the provision of short breaks or respite care is very patchy across the country. Some parents may have as little as one 'tea time' each month as their short break, this being their only respite from the responsibility of caring for a child or young person with SEN or a disability. Schools should be sensitive to the pressure this constant responsibility places on families, especially where there are other children, or particularly in the case of a single parent.

Where short breaks are a regular feature of a pupil's life, it is beneficial for the school to have some communication with the respite carers whether that care happens in a specialist centre or as a short-term foster care arrangement. Pupils may show their anxieties around transferring from one home setting to another through different behaviours in school. Communication between the short-break carers and school staff, and the use of familiar systems and routines, will minimise these anxieties. Share with short-break carers the pupil's learning objectives and any other strategies used in school, such as a few signs or a symbol communication board. This continuity of approach will help the pupil to settle in the different environment and better understand that they are cared for and safe in all settings.

The school will need to prepare the pupil for any changes necessary to transport arrangements because of short breaks. A different driver or a change of escort can cause some pupils severe anxiety and lead to great upset and changes in behaviour. Encourage the pupil to take a favourite book or game with him or her in the transport, a sort of 'short-break treat' that will make the occasion more special and less scary. Explain to the pupil how long it will be before he or she returns home. A simple day chart made of card on which the pupil crosses off as each day as it passes will help him or her gauge how long they will be away, and to understand that they have not been abandoned forever.

Monday	Tuesday	Wednesday	Thursday	Friday
Home	Home	Claire's	Claire's	Home

Figure 3.1 Short-break timeline

Life skills issues

Personal hygiene

When some pupils with SEND enter secondary school, they may still have some difficulties using the toilet or keeping themselves clean. This is not – and should not be allowed to become – a big deal. The more anxious a pupil feels about using the toilet, the greater the difficulties will become. It is often the minutiae of a situation that cause most problems. Questions such as:

'Who should pay for the wet wipes to enable a pupil to clean himself independently?'

or:

'Is it OK for an adult go into the toilet cubicle with the pupil?'

are often stumbling blocks. These things should be discussed and are then easily sorted out with families.

When a pupil has particular long-term difficulties with using the toilet effectively, take a pragmatic approach and teach him or her to be as independent as possible, but accept that they might need occasional support if they are ill or in a different setting.

Eating and drinking

Pupils with SEND may have associated problems with eating and drinking. These problems may take the form of:

- *Constant hunger*: where the pupil has no 'full- up' sensation and so feels hungry all the time. Pupils with this difficulty are not just being greedy. Ask parents to put additional nutritious snacks into a lunchbox, especially foods that take longer to eat, such as an apple or a carrot and ensure that all subject teachers allow the pupil to eat when he or she needs to. Frequent opportunities to eat small amounts of food will help the pupil to concentrate on their work rather than on when they can next eat.
- *A restricted diet*: Most children go through a phase of being fussy eaters but some pupils with SEND (and especially those children with Autistic Spectrum Disorder) may persist in eating only a very restricted and repetitive diet. This diet may take the form of insisting on eating the same food for every meal, such as pizza or sausage and chips. This may not be a healthy diet but the pupil is likely to be getting most essential nutrients. It is when pupils will eat only such foods as crisps or dry bread that long-term health concerns arise. This is a potential battle best left to families to resolve. In school pupils should not be coerced into eating foods they find unpalatable, as coercion may set up distressing negative connotations, and could lead to him or her refusing to come to school. If school is concerned because the pupil is losing weight, or appears unwell, this should be discussed with parents.

Multi-agency involvement

The panoply of medical and social work professionals that opens up following the birth of a child with SEND is daunting for any new parents. By the time the pupil starts secondary school the swathe of education professionals will be significant: educational psychologists, local authority officers, teachers, teaching assistants, etc. In listening to all these people, some of whom are eminent in their field, parents have to decide on the best course of action for their own child. In particular, doctors often advise parents very early in a child's life that placement in a special school would be best. This is because doctors necessarily see the disability as the priority, rather than the child as a whole, and they may have little understanding or experience of how a child with more significant special educational needs can be educated successfully in mainstream schools.

Parents must be given the necessary information, but all the agencies involved with a child must work together to give parents a coherent and thorough understanding of their child's needs. As far as possible, parents should be enabled to manage the process themselves, and be given copies of all reports so that they can read them in their own time and make decisions based on all the information available.

The language of reports

The professionals who make up multi-agency teams are all highly educated people, and each professional group has its own terminology and 'shorthand phrases', or jargon. This jargon can carry over into the language used in meetings and in written reports. Comments such as:

'He has externalised his locus of control.'

or:

'She has delayed expressive and receptive language skills.'

may mean nothing to parents (nor most likely to the other professionals). Parents are entitled to both written and verbal information in a form they can easily understand. This also ensures that all professionals are able to work together more directly and effectively. This is not to recommend 'talking down' to parents, but endorses the sharing of clear and accurate information accessible to all.

Assessment/test results

The need for clarity also extends to sharing with parents the results of tests or other assessments. Professionals look at a series of figures and, through experience, can draw out the meaning and relevance, but parents cannot do this. Written or spoken in plain language, a coherent summary of the results allows parents to understand and ask questions. Important, potentially life-changing decisions often rest on test results, and parents deserve and should expect full understanding and involvement.

Collaboration with other professionals

A significant step forward is made when all professionals work across disciplines, each accepting and respecting the expertise of the others, and all working within a shared common concern for the child or young person as a learner. In this way team roles are not fixed, nor are there clear boundaries between disciplines.

For example, a speech and language therapist works in the classroom during an English lesson with a small group of pupils, including pupils with EHC plans. This work is based on the learning objectives for the whole group, and the shared communication objectives from the EHC plans. The therapist also trains and monitors the work of those teaching assistants in the school who support a number of pupils with speech and language difficulties. The programmes devised are based on and woven throughout the curriculum, rather than being 'bolt-ons' that require pupils to be withdrawn. The therapist joins the English faculty team meetings and feels sufficiently confident to make suggestions about teaching and learning strategies that go beyond language and communication.

Other ways to develop collaboration across disciplines

- A SENCO and parents working with a paediatrician to monitor the effects of a particular drug regime.
- Speech and language therapists advising on the curriculum to promote a language-rich environment across all subjects.
- Occupational therapists advising on the furniture in classrooms, or having an input into the PE scheme of work.
- A team of teachers, parents, social workers and specialist nurses from the Children and Adolescents Mental Health Service (CAMHS) collaborating on a social skills programme across the school.
- Parents, educational psychologists, teachers, speech and language therapists, occupational therapists and parents working together to devise an holistic programme of education and care for a pupil.

Collaboration across disciplines at this 'shop floor' level helps parents to see how everyone is working together in the best interest of their children.

SEND review meetings

The SEND Code of Practice 2015 (6.65, p. 104) states that teachers should meet with the parents of children and young people with SEND at least three times a year to discuss the pupil's learning and wider development. These termly reviews will, in the context of the objectives for the end of the school year and the long-term outcomes for the end of the key stage, focus on the short-term targets for which the pupil is aiming. Evidence from the pilot of the Achievement for All programme shows how effective well-structured, termly conversations about a pupil's learning can be both to improve the engagement of parents but, more significantly, to drive progress beyond that previously expected. The purposes of the Achievement for All structured conversation are to:

- establish an effective relationship between parents and a key teacher;
- allow the parents an opportunity to share their concerns and together agree their aspirations for their child;
- set clear goals and targets for learning and improvement in wider outcomes such as attendance, behaviour and participation in extra-curricular activities;
- determine activities which will contribute to the achievement of those targets;
- identify the responsibilities of the parent, the pupil and the school;
- agree the date and time of the next meeting;
- clarify the most effective means of communication between meetings.

In the pilot programme the termly conversations with parents and the pupil were structured into four sections: *explore, focus, plan and review*.

- *Explore*: where the teacher uses the skills of active listening, paraphrasing and summarising to find out what the parents want and aspire for their child; what needs the pupil has, what strategies have worked in the past either at home or in an earlier stage of education; and what is getting in the way of the pupil's achievement.

- *Focus*: where the teacher helps the parents to identify the key issues and priorities for action.
- *Plan*: to address the key issues and priorities the planning stage is concerned with the actions necessary. The parents and teacher set and agree aspirational targets that create a framework against which progress can be measured.
- *Review*: in the review stage the teacher summarises the conversation for the parents and the pupil, agrees next steps, and organises the ongoing communication between home and school.

(*Achievement for All: Structured Conversation Handbook to Support Learning*, 2009, p. 9)

This framework is echoed in the 2015 SEND Code of Practice which states 'discussions with parents should be structured in such a way that they develop a good understanding of the pupil's areas of strength and difficulty, the parents' concerns, the agreed outcomes sought for the child and the next steps' (Section 6.39, p. 99).

Some parents find it helpful to have a comments sheet to fill in before the meeting. This encourages them to note down and remember to ask the questions *they* feel are important, rather than fitting to the school's agenda.

Setting and reviewing learning targets

Focus on outcomes

The higher the aspirations we have for pupils with SEND, and that they have for themselves, the more he or she will achieve. As we focus more on the pupil's desired outcomes, and to give the pupil a good chance of achieving them, so the short-term targets agreed by the pupil, parents and teachers will need to be sufficiently aspirational. This compels us to look beyond the next step in learning towards a trajectory for achievement. Both outcomes and learning targets are intended to define clearly what a pupil is expected to know and/or do as a result of instruction – i.e., the benefit the pupil will derive from an intervention or programme of instruction. For example, Ross is in Year 7. One of Ross's outcomes is that by the time he leaves secondary school he will communicate and interact with familiar people, and join in with social activities in college. To support Ross's progress towards this outcome his parents and key teacher together have agreed a target for the next twelve weeks; Ross will ask questions and respond appropriately to questions from other people. To support Ross to achieve this target he will play a battleships game with friends three times each week in school, and once at home at the weekend with his parents and brother.

The effectiveness of the learning targets should also be reviewed and evaluated. If the pupil is not making the progress expected, then that is not necessarily the his or her fault; either the targets or the intervention are not appropriate, or support is not effective. Either way, the response to a lack of progress should be to do something different and review more frequently. Any specific difficulties that impact on the child's learning, such as problems with physical access or accessing the curriculum, should be discussed. New targets and future action can be agreed at the meeting, and the roles of parents, school and the child clearly set out.

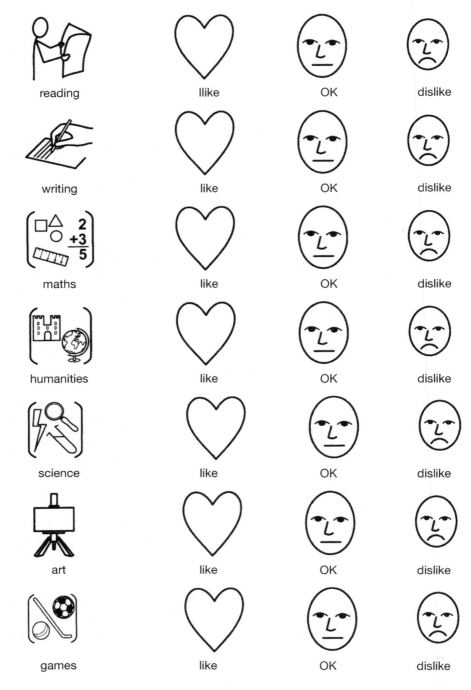

reading	like	OK	dislike
writing	like	OK	dislike
maths	like	OK	dislike
humanities	like	OK	dislike
science	like	OK	dislike
art	like	OK	dislike
games	like	OK	dislike

Figure 3.2 SEN review pupil feedback form

© 2016 *Meeting Special Educational Needs in Secondary Classrooms*, Sue Briggs, Routledge

Framework for the SEND review meeting

1   Welcome to parents and pupil. Discuss:

- the pupil's view of progress;
- the parents' view of progress;
- the teacher's view of progress.

2   How effective have the previous learning targets been?
3   Updated or new information and/or advice.
4   What additional measures need to be taken to ensure access to the school and curriculum?
5   Revised targets and support at school and at home.
6   Any other questions.

Annual review meetings

For pupils with an EHC plan, LAs have a statutory duty to arrange a meeting with parents at least once a year to review the plan. The annual review ensures that the parents, the pupil, the LA, the school, and all the professionals involved consider the progress the pupil has made over the previous year; and whether amendments need to be made to the outcomes, the description of the pupil's needs, or to the special educational provision specified in the plan. The EHC plan should be at the heart of this meeting and all those present must have a copy. This meeting is different from the SEN review meetings that are held three times a year, but may replace one of those meetings.

Parents and all the professionals involved with the pupil will be invited both to send a report and to attend the meeting. Parents new to the annual review system may expect all the professionals from outside the school to attend the meeting, and can be very disappointed when they find it is just themselves and school staff. Let parents know in advance that professionals from outside school such as educational psychologists or occupational therapists, usually only attend annual reviews before major transitions, or if significant changes are to be made to the plan.

When a large number of professionals are to attend the meeting, make sure parents know well in advance exactly who will be there and who will be chairing the meeting. Offer a pre-meeting between the parents and SENCO, or the form tutor, so that together they can prepare any questions. Difficult issues can be raised and discussed in this more informal setting, such as whether parents wish their child to attend the meeting. Allow parents to bring a friend or family member to give them support at the meeting. This is especially important for a single parent, or if only one parent is able to attend.

Effective communication between home and school should mean that there are no surprises for parents at this meeting. Any potentially distressing or difficult information should be given to parents, and explained thoroughly well before the date of the meeting.

It is useful to send out a simple agenda at least a week prior to the meeting. This should list the areas to be discussed so that parents know what is going to happen, and when.

At the meeting:

- The form tutor or SENCO should welcome the parents and pupil and escort them to the meeting room. When the parents are settled and ready, the professionals are invited to enter the meeting room and asked to introduce themselves, explaining their role and the reason for their being at the meeting.
- If the pupil is not to attend all of the meeting, give everyone present a copy of his or her current one-page profile. This keeps the pupil at the forefront of the discussion and provides everyone with current information about the pupil, and his or her aspirations and preferences.
- Always invite parents to speak first and allow them the final word at the end. If parents are reluctant to speak, encourage them gently as they must feel they have had their say. If they do not feel that, they are likely to become disillusioned and negative.
- No new diagnoses, test results or major changes to provision should ever be brought up in annual review meetings without parents having been given this information privately beforehand. Sudden revelations are unfair to parents and will ruin any trust built up over time. If communication between home and school is working as it should, the meeting should simply build on and consolidate information already shared and discussed.

Working with siblings

The siblings of pupils with SEND will each have their own ways of coming to terms with having a brother or sister with special needs or a disability. Having a sibling with SEND in the same school should not in itself make the situation more difficult, although some parents do prefer their children to be in different schools. This is usually because parents fear that the sibling might feel they have to take responsibility for a sister or brother with SEND. Schools must be cautious neither to expect nor to allow siblings to take on this responsibility; they should be treated just the same as all other brothers and sisters would be in school.

There will inevitably be comparisons between siblings. A much younger child might outstrip their big brother or sister academically, and the child with SEND may lose self-esteem and their role as older sibling. Where this is the case, endeavour to boost the status of the older child within the school by giving responsibilities or praising his/her other skills and qualities, such as being a good friend.

Sisters and brothers of children with SEND must be allowed the freedom to develop in their own right, and not just as Peter's or Sarah's brother. Some young people will have a great sense of responsibility towards their brother or sister, and school will need to be careful that the sibling does not take on the role of minder. Equally, some pupils will make every effort to have no contact with their siblings in school time.

Should the pupil with SEND become ill or develop a secondary condition such as epilepsy, a strong and trusting ongoing relationship with parents will be a huge bonus for the whole family. During periods of illness the parents must focus on the sick child, and other children may be worried about their sibling but might also feel left out. Teachers and teaching assistants can help through these times by giving a pupil opportunities to talk about the situation at home in a relaxed and informal way. Pupils can carry a huge amount of anxiety, often thinking that they might be to blame in some way, and a quiet chat during a break or over lunch can ease that burden.

Summary

Parents are the real experts on their own children. When the professionals have gone home from work parents once again take on that life-long responsibility.

Working with parents brings benefits for pupils and for the school. A teacher or teaching assistant in a secondary school is a very important part of a child's life, and their actions and opinions will affect the whole family. Keep the channels of communication open, especially during difficult periods or disagreement, and you can share all the challenges and successes, and will feel less anxious about meeting the pupil's needs.

Chapter 4 gives teachers advice and support for planning the inclusive curriculum.

Chapter 4

Planning and teaching the curriculum for inclusion

In any mainstream year group there will always be several pupils operating at earlier stages of the National Curriculum than the majority of their peers. Even where pupils work in sets there will remain a significant minority struggling with basic skills. This chapter will give teachers ideas on how to make the secondary curriculum more inclusive for pupils with SEND without creating a mountain of extra work.

Planning for classes that include pupils with SEND is sometimes daunting, and teachers can be put off even before they start. It really doesn't have to be complicated, nor need it create a great deal of additional work. The key is not to write a completely different scheme of work for one or two pupils. You can adapt the planning systems you have already. However, planning for pupils with SEND is impossible to do 'on the hoof'; it needs to be done in advance at the same time as the planning for the rest of the group. Keep an extra piece of paper on one side as you plan your lessons, and as opportunities for differentiation arise, write them down.

It is vital to have high expectations of all pupils even, or especially, for those with SEND.

Often teachers feel the best way to plan for a pupil with SEND is to look for workbooks or materials suitable for the pupil's academic ability level. In effect, this means the pupil working through primary workbooks with a teaching assistant, with the work undertaken having no connection to that of the rest of the class. In this sort of situation the pupil with SEND may rarely have any attention from the teacher, resulting in him or her being 'minded' rather than being taught.

New learning should be teacher-led, with teaching assistants supporting the pupils in practising and consolidating the skills and knowledge.

Schools are constantly bombarded with advertisements for new and better materials for pupils with special needs. New sets of books or software promise to sort out the planning and meet pupil needs, but all too often they do not. In fact, a teacher's brains and creativity are far superior to any new software or textbook. Try to ignore the blandishments of advertising. Totally different resources and activities are not necessary. The answers are rarely found in new resources no matter how glossy the catalogue or impressive the claim. Talent, creativity and experience among teachers and teaching assistants are the most powerful factors in determining and meeting pupils' needs so as to help them make progress.

Case study: Omar

Omar is in Year 8. His reading is at a very early stage of development. He worked on the Oxford Reading Tree scheme until the end of Year 7, but became reluctant to keep on trying, and he was bored with books that he felt were too babyish. Omar finds word building very difficult but he can remember some words which have direct relevance to him and his life. His teaching assistant has helped him create a series of books about his family, his friends and his special interests, such as helping his father with jobs in the garden and the workshop, and lorries. Each book has the same format, with photographs and a word or short phrase underneath. Omar's family were involved in making the books, with his father photographing Omar working in the garden and in the workshop and then sending the pictures to school. The books are kept in school, but Omar frequently takes them home to share with his family. This work has motivated Omar to learn to read a significant number of new words. The amount of text in each book can be increased as Omar's reading develops.

Targets and progress

No matter how excellent the teaching and the care given, pupils with SEND can sometimes fall behind their peers in academic development. The gap may become increasingly wide as the pupils get older, but experience from recent research, most specifically the pilot programme of Achievement for All, proves that this widening of the gap is not inevitable. Some secondary schools in that pilot were so successful that many of the pupils with SEND in the target year groups made accelerated progress and achieved results well beyond what was expected. The factors in this success were threefold:

1   Access to high quality teaching, including effective tracking and evidence-based interventions.
2   Partnership with parents: teachers and parents together discussing learning and agreeing targets, and with families supported with advice and materials to develop their children's learning at home and for wider outcomes.
3   Support to improve attendance and behaviour, reduce bullying, and offer greater participation in the full life of the school including extra-curricular activities.

(Achievement for All: Guidance for Schools, 2009)

None of these factors are new to schools, but when brought to bear for pupils with SEND, the combined effect of them was profound. The concept used for target setting in the Achievement for All pilot was that of 'accelerated progress', an expectation that children with SEND would not only make expected progress but would begin to catch up lost ground – and they did!

Aspirations, outcomes, objectives and targets

All children and young people have aspirations for the future – e.g., to get a good job, to travel the world, to have more leisure time. The aspirations of children with SEND can offer us the context on which to develop motivational learning targets and activities. Take Philip, who at age 11 was determined to become a cricket scorer. Philip had a severe communication disability (semantic pragmatic language disorder), which made social interaction and the development of numeracy skills very difficult for him. His communication difficulties were certainly a barrier for him, but barriers that Philip, his family and his school were determined to overcome. By offering Philip tasks linked to cricket and cricket scoring, his teachers were able to maintain his motivation to learn, and, at age 14 he began to score for the school team and at 16 for the local amateur team. As an adult, Philip achieved his ambition by scoring for the county cricket club near his home.

Philip's aspiration was ambitious for him, but some children and young people have aspirations that seem completely unattainable – to be an astronaut or to climb Everest. Whatever a pupil's aspiration, it is real and relevant for him or her, and we must not take that away. Rather, we can use the aspiration as a starting point for planning with the pupil and his or her parents what outcomes the pupil will need to achieve to get at least some of the way towards the goal.

Outcomes

The Children and Families Act 2014 and SEND Code of Practice 2015 introduce the concept of 'outcomes' for children and young people with SEND. The definition of an outcome is 'the benefit or difference made to an individual as a result of an intervention' (SEND Code of Practice, 2015, 3.31, p. 46). An outcome should be something over which those involved have control and influence, it should be SMART – Specific, Measurable, Achievable, Realistic and Time-bound – and should usually set out what needs to be achieved by the end of a phase or stage of education.

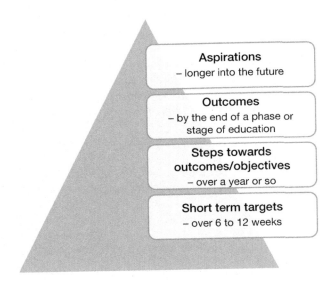

Figure 4.1 Aspirations and outcomes diagram

Objectives: steps towards outcomes

We can maintain a direct link with the pupil's aspirations by making yearly objectives the steps towards the desired outcomes. Objectives over a year or so also fit well with the annual review of EHC plans and give a firm basis on which to set short-term targets to be achieved over a few weeks or a term. It is important to remember that setting effective objectives requires skill, and must focus on something that the pupil will achieve or a skill to be developed, rather than provision that he or she will receive. For example, Adya is in the final term of Year 8 and her objective was written as 'Adya will work with Mrs Balyan on her English targets three times each week for twenty minutes'. However, as Adya's mum pointed out, this is actually a description of the provision that the school will provide for Adya. What her English teacher and her parents wanted Adya to reach over the next year would actually be 'to improve her reading and writing skills to the level that she can access the curriculum in Key Stage 4', and this is what was finally agreed as one of her objectives.

Short-term targets

Short-term learning targets are the real drivers of progress in classrooms and real skill is required to set relevant aspirational targets. Just as with the yearly objectives, targets must focus on the expected impact of whatever intervention is used to help the pupil with SEND to make good or better progress.

Short-term subject targets that are understood by and agreed with the pupil with SEND and their parents during the SEN Review Conversations will provide an effective means of measuring progress over time. Make the targets visible by sticking them in the front of an exercise book or on a bookmark and refer to them at the start and end of every lesson.

It is very important to track the progress of pupils with SEND most carefully so that the impact of and their response to all activities and interventions is understood; should progress falter, adaptations then can be made. Often schools persist with an intervention even when the pupil is no longer making the anticipated progress, or even making no progress at all. If an intervention is not enabling the pupil to make the anticipated progress it is either the wrong intervention or it is being delivered incorrectly. Either way, it isn't the pupil's fault that he or she is making no progress. If an intervention hasn't had an impact after six weeks it is unlikely to be successful after twelve weeks. No pupil can afford to waste twelve weeks on something that isn't working, much less a pupil with SEND. Don't be frightened to admit that an intervention hasn't worked – ditch it and try something else.

For children with more complex SEND, it is important, of course, to celebrate all achievement no matter how small the step. But by setting only small-step, easily achievable targets, are we condemning children and young people always to fall behind? Challenging though it may be, it is better to set targets that offer a high level of aspiration and ambition, because pupils frequently do meet these challenges. Targets should be set that at the very least have an expectation of the pupil achieving the objectives and outcomes agreed for the end of the school year or the key stage.

Incorporating objectives from other agencies

External agencies such as speech and language therapy or occupational therapy commonly work in close co-operation with teachers and support staff in mainstream secondary schools. The system of withdrawing pupils from class for therapy is now usually replaced by the therapists assessing pupils' communication needs and then working with teachers to plan activities to be carried out in school, the therapists checking on progress and adjusting the programme. So therapy objectives are incorporated into pupils' individual learning targets. Therapists also offer training to whole-school or faculty teams so that a more communication-rich environment is developed that benefits all pupils.

Where there is a strong and professional relationship between therapist and school, this consultation model is more effective than the isolated 20 minutes of therapy each week. It makes better use of the therapist's time, and develops valuable skills for teachers and teaching assistants which may be used with other pupils. Parents are often wary of this system, particularly where the pupil has therapy time specified on his/her EHC plan. Good communication between therapist, school and parents is necessary to help parents understand that their child is actually receiving better and more effective therapy. Invite the therapist to join part of the SEND Review Conversation where progress in communication can be discussed openly, and offer parents the opportunity to observe the daily therapy programme in practice. In this way, parents can be helped to feel part of the therapy process and their confidence in the provision will develop.

When planning to include a pupil with SEND in your subject lessons liaise with the therapists and the SENCO to see if there are therapy objectives that might link in with particular topics or units of work. Physiotherapy targets can be addressed in PE and games, occupational therapy targets in art and design and technology, and speech and language therapy targets in English and drama. In this way the impact of therapy will be consolidated and amplified without the pupil being withdrawn from class activities.

Some schools are reluctant to accept on their roll what they perceive as 'more than their fair share' of pupils with SEND because of the potential impact on their GCSE results.

However, the old adage of measuring what we value, rather than valuing what we can measure, holds true for pupils with SEND. If a school as a whole values and celebrates all pupil achievements academic or otherwise, the entire community is lifted and energised. Life is about more than GCSEs, and good schools develop and celebrate achievements in all aspects of the curriculum, academic and affective.

Tracking back to success

For some pupils with SEND in mainstream classrooms, tracking back is the most effective method of setting appropriate learning objectives. This approach is effective during Key Stage 3 when planning for pupils with SEND who are working well below age-related expectations. The assumption behind the approach is that all pupils, no matter what their level of attainment, should work within a class of their chronological peers.

The starting point for including pupils with SEND is the objective from the National Curriculum programme of study for the whole class. Once the class objective has been decided, the teacher tracks back through the programme of study for his or her subject to an earlier stage to find a related objective for the pupil with SEND. Working through the tracking back process with a teaching assistant who knows the pupil well will ensure the objective is appropriate for the individual, and will spark off ideas for activities and resources. This knowledge is very important in helping to decide on appropriate teaching strategies and questioning styles that will motivate individual pupils to learn.

For some pupils it will be necessary to track back into previous key stages. Aim to identify relevant objectives that will challenge pupils, but which are pitched at an appropriate and realistic level. This will ensure that pupils experience the full range of the curriculum while working on objectives appropriate to their individual needs.

Take into account the different ways that pupils learn and use this information to influence your choice of teaching strategies. Next, write down anything else you wish to improve, or to teach the pupil in the context of your subject lesson. For instance:

- turn taking;
- working independently;
- being responsible for collecting his or her own equipment.

These aspects may form the basis for a pupil's work for a series of lessons covering academic, personal and social objectives.

Tracking back during the planning process for each half term means the teacher can plan shared activities for all pupils in the class, rather than designing completely separate activities for pupils with SEND. The concept of pupils working on individually appropriate objectives within a shared activity is a powerful and effective way of including pupils with a diverse range of learning needs. While tracking back is appropriate for pupils with SEND, tracking forward may be appropriate for more able pupils.

The very important final step is to return to the age-appropriate objective to prepare the context in which to set the learning. This last step is vital if pupils are to experience the challenge of a broadening curriculum as they move through the school.

Once the objectives and activities for the lessons have been planned, a teaching assistant could further support the process by collecting any additional resources before each lesson and recording pupils' responses. This recording then informs future planning. A sample recording form is included here.

Name: Class/Year group: Subject:

Date	Lesson objectives	Resources	Responses	Next steps	TA

Figure 4.2 Template for pupil response recording form

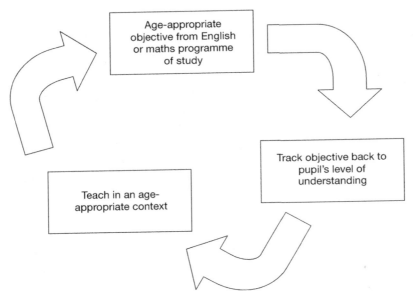

Figure 4.3 Tracking back diagram

Tracking back: in short

1   Tracking back takes place at the medium-term planning stage.
2   Start from the age-appropriate objectives in the National Curriculum programme of study for your subject.
3   Track back through the programme of study to an objective appropriate to the needs of the pupil with SEND, but always include an element of challenge to the work. Work that is too easy is just as demoralizing as tasks that are too difficult.
4   Return to the age-appropriate part of the programme of study as this is the context in which the objective will be taught.
5   Identify class and group activities that address the objectives of all the class, *and* the pupils with SEND.

The key concepts method

The key concepts method works particularly well in subjects such as history, geography, PSHE and RE. Once again, the starting point is the class objective. Identify three or four key concepts which you want the pupil or pupils with SEND to know – the key concepts of the lesson. For example, in history a Year 8 history group learn about the English Civil War as part of a series of lessons focusing on the development of Church, State and society in Britain, 1509–1745.

The key concepts for a pupil with SEND could be:

- The Civil War was over 300 years ago.
- Charles I was beheaded.
- Cromwell was Lord Protector.

In addressing these concepts the lesson will also develop important skills such as the ability to identify significant events, make connections, draw contrasts and analyse trends over long periods of time.

Planning for the class as a whole is then much easier. The teacher plans the lesson and incorporates a variety of activities and resources that addresses the key concepts in addition to the class objectives. Pupils with SEND are enabled to participate, working

Case study: Yasmina

An example of the key concepts method

Pupils in a Year 7 geography class are working on a series of lessons based the Key Stage 3 programme of study.

The learning outcome for the whole class is:

- To understand the concept of a 'geographical hierarchy'. For this lesson the learning objectives are:

  - To think of a house, street, city, country, continent as a geographical unit.
  - To know that a place and its location can be shown using a variety of maps and photographs.

Based on this objective, the teacher and teaching assistant identified two key concepts of the lesson for Yasmina:

- To know her own home address, and
- to identify her home and street on photographs and a local map.

The teacher and TA prepared activities for the lesson that involved Yasmina working in a small group, then with a teaching assistant, and finally with one other pupil.

The first activity involved small groups of pupils looking at photographs of their homes and the local area. The group discussed the images and Yasmina was able to identify her home and some of the buildings.

Yasmina then worked with a teaching assistant. They looked at photographs of buildings familiar to Yasmina – her home, a supermarket, a petrol station, the post office, the mosque, etc. Together they made a book about the town and the familiar landmarks. They included information on where Yasmina's parents worked, the transport she used to travel to school, and the mosque where her family worshipped. Yasmina used a tablet computer to write the captions for the book. Yasmina then played a lotto game with a partner, matching OS symbols to photographs. After the game, she stuck the symbols into her geography book.

Name: Kuli	Class/Year group: 8LS	Subject: History	Teacher: Mr Rashid	Other adult/s: Mr Collins	
	Support	**Grouping**	**Resources**	**Recording**	**Key Knowledge**
Activity 1 Introduction (10 minutes)	Peer support from Katie (talk partners). Mr Collins on same table.	Pair and table group	Small whiteboard for each pair 'Listen' symbol as reminder when teacher speaking List of key words	n/a	The development of church, state and society in Britain 1509–1745 • The English Civil War was over 300 years ago • Charles I was beheaded • Cromwell was Lord Protector
Activity 2 Create article for front page of newspaper about death of King Charles I (20 minutes)	Mr Rashid and group	Group of 4 (mixed-ability)	Camera Flipchart paper Marker pens	Camera	
					Key Words
Activity 3 Clicker 6 activity on laptop (20 minutes)	Mr Collins and Joseph	Paired work with Joseph	Clicker 6 software	Printout of finished work	Past Civil War
Activity 4 Plenary (10 minutes)	Peer support from Katie (talk partners). Mr Collins on same table.	Pair and table group	Small whiteboard for each pair 'Listen' symbol as reminder when teacher speaking List of key words Homework task slip to be put in planner	Pair self-assessment of learning on whiteboards	Parliament King Cromwell

Figure 4.4a Example of a completed lesson differentiation planner

	Support	Grouping	Resources	Recording	Key Knowledge
Activity 1					
Activity 2					
Activity 3					Key Words
Activity 4					

Name: _____   Class/Year group: _____   Subject: _____   Teacher: _____   Other adult/s: _____

Figure 4.4b Template for lesson differentiation planner

in groups or in pairs. The sharp focus of two or three key concepts makes assessment much easier, and pupils learn more effectively when they know what is expected of them. As the key concepts are a part of what everyone else in the class is learning, they can be shared during the introduction to the lesson – written on the whiteboard or at the top of a worksheet – and referred to again at points throughout the lesson to check that the concepts are understood.

The planning of lessons so as to make key concepts accessible ensures that the amount and level of information matches the pupil's ability and understanding. Without this approach, in an undifferentiated lesson the sheer quantity of information, and the level of complexity of both the verbal and written language will overwhelm pupils with SEND. They cannot access such lessons at any level.

Key concepts: in short

The teacher and teaching assistant together should:

- Prepare the class objectives for the lesson.
- Look at the National Curriculum programmes of study in the subject that matches the ability of the pupil with SEND.
- Identify two or three key concepts from the class outcomes/objectives at an appropriately challenging level for the pupil with SEND.
- Plan the lesson, incorporating group and individual activities that address the key concepts.
- Prepare any additional resources.
- Share the key concepts with the whole class.
- Return to key concepts throughout and at the end of the lesson to check understanding.
- Assess against the key concepts after each lesson.

Curriculum overlapping

The majority of pupils with SEND need to spend additional school time working on communication, reading, writing and maths targets from Individual Education Plans. Often in a mainstream secondary school it is neither possible nor desirable to withdraw pupils from class to work on these basic skills. For pupils with more complex learning difficulties, an approach that allows these skills to be developed in subject lessons alongside other pupils is curriculum overlapping (Doyle and Giangreco, 2013, p. 68; Giangreco et al., 1998).

In curriculum overlapping, the pupil with SEND joins in all lessons with his or her chronological age group. For some lessons, the pupil with SEND focuses on his or her individual literacy or numeracy targets, while the rest of the class work on the subject objectives in, for example, history, geography, music or biology. The context for the learning is the subject area. The pupil with SEND is still expected to work in groups or with a partner.

Curriculum overlapping must be developed by the SENCO, subject teachers and teaching assistants working together as a team. There needs to be careful planning to give the pupil opportunities to address his or her individual learning targets while maintaining the entitlement to a broad and balanced curriculum.

Box 4.1 Examples of curriculum overlapping

Josef

Josef is in Year 9. He has Williams syndrome. He has good expressive language but his comprehension is comparatively delayed. Josef has a reading age of 6 years and 5 months. His current learning target for writing is:

Josef will write two- or three-word captions to match pictures.

The Year 9 biology class is learning about the content of a healthy human diet: carbohydrates, fats, proteins, vitamins, minerals, dietary fibre and water, and why each is needed. One of the learning objectives for the class is to be able to classify foods into different nutrient groups. To address both the biology outcome and Josef's learning targets, the teacher devises a food lotto game using words and pictures. Josef plays a simplified version of the game with a partner and then writes a short sentence for each picture using a laptop with Clicker 6 software.

Curriculum overlapping can also be used to address other individual learning targets. For example:

Poppy

Poppy's learning targets include one for behaviour, as she finds it very difficult to sit still and concentrate for more than five minutes at a time. In the same biology lesson, Poppy is working on the target 'Poppy will stay in her seat and on task for 10 minutes'. The context in which she is working is a Year 9 biology lesson but it is the individual behaviour target that will be the focus of the lesson and assessment for Poppy.

Making connections

The ability to generalise information from one context to another is for many pupils with SEND an area of particular weakness. Even where they show understanding and attainment in one context it cannot be assumed that they will be able to use that understanding and knowledge in a different context. For example, a pupil may be able to weigh amounts in grams in maths lessons, but may need to be taught the skill again in food technology.

Where possible, find and build on links with other subjects to help pupils generalise information across subjects. Make those links explicit. Remind the pupil what they have learned previously and show them the relevant page in their book or folder. In each lesson take a photograph of the pupil with SEND, either holding an object related to the topic, or involved in an activity. This will help him or her to remember the lesson and to begin to make the necessary links to other areas of the curriculum.

Discrete subject lessons in secondary schools do not easily lend themselves to links between the different areas of the curriculum, with the possible exceptions of literacy and numeracy. However, all pupils benefit when cross-curricular themes can be identified and links made explicit.

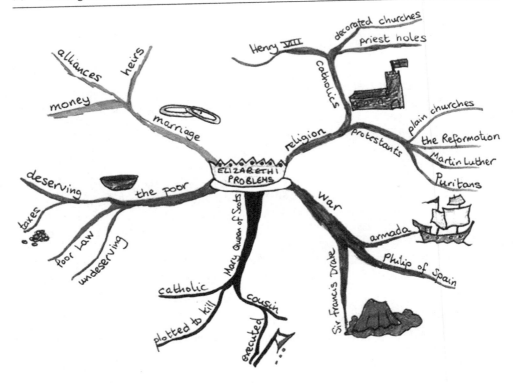

Figure 4.5 Concept map

Concept maps

Concept maps are a valuable way of making visual links between subjects and information (Buzan, 2010). A concept map is made up of words, colours, lines and/or pictures. The map helps pupils to organise their thinking and to remember information. An adult can create the concept map if the pupil is not able to do it for him- or herself. The use of different colours, shapes, pictures and even photographs supports learning and aids memory. Keep the maps clear and simple, or they will add to the pupil's confusion.

Revisiting concepts

After only one lesson pupils with SEND may find it difficult to learn and retain information. They will need opportunities to revisit concepts several times and in different situations. The old army sergeant adage of 'Tell 'em what you're going to tell 'em; tell them; then tell 'em what you've just told 'em', describes just the right approach for pupils with SEND.

Make the objective clear at the start of the lesson so they know what they are going to learn. Teach the concept through a variety of activities and with a range of resources, then go back to the objective to show the pupil what they have learned.

Multisensory learning

The traditional 'chalk and talk' type of lesson will exclude many pupils who have a more visual or kinaesthetic preferred mode of learning, any pupils with hearing loss or visual impairment, and those with learning or communication difficulties. This will encompass a significant group of pupils in every class, particularly in the winter months when even a bad cold can significantly reduce acuity of hearing. A sensory impairment does not need to be severe to have a profound impact on learning – an out of date or dirty pair of prescription spectacles will, for example, limit a student's vision.

Most pupils benefit from teaching styles which maximise multisensory involvement but, by the time pupils reach secondary school, many lessons are predominantly sedentary with the emphasis on auditory information and writing tasks. In the Foundation Stage and Key Stage 1, the curriculum is founded on play-based learning, with practical activities giving children the opportunity to explore through all senses. They are encouraged to run, climb, stretch, roll and explore the world around them. Throughout the primary and secondary phase, however, the amount of exploration and practical activity gradually diminishes until largely it is limited to drama, PE, and design and technology lessons. Some pupils, even as teenagers and young adults, need more activity and it is unreasonable to expect some of them to sit still for fifty minutes or an hour at a time.

Variation and pace

Our students are used to receiving information from the media in short, sharp bites. Varied activities in short bursts make lessons more interesting and memorable, but the rapid pace of some lessons serves to exclude certain pupils; those with SEND, those with communication difficulties, those with attention disorders, and those with sensory impairments. It is important for lessons to have pace, but the same pace does not need to be maintained throughout. Vary the pace and break up the lesson into shorter activities, and you will help all pupils to improve the inclusion of those with any learning problems.

Change the seating arrangements and give pupils the chance to stand for a while or change position. Where sitting behind a desk for the whole lesson cannot be avoided, give pupils the chance to stand up, move around and stretch at least twice.

Practical experiences and apparatus

When planning to include pupils with SEND, identify every possible opportunity for them to use practical, hands-on equipment and engage in first-hand experiences. Abstract concepts will likely not be understood unless linked to real-life, concrete examples and experiences. They might hear about wind power in science, but to understand it they need to feel the force of the wind for themselves. Let them fly a kite, hold a windsock, or just walk across the playing field on a windy day.

If a maths class is working on fractions, give the pupil with SEND a piece of card to cut into halves, quarters and eighths. Teachers sometimes find that the practical activities throw up challenging questions. In a lesson on 2-D shape, a pupil would not accept the plastic shapes that were offered. She insisted that the shapes were 3-D because she could see the 1 millimetre edges. How thin does a 3-D shape have to be to become 2-D? Not the kind of philosophical question one would expect from a pupil with SEND, but often they bring fresh perspectives that challenge assumptions.

Other sensory cues

One sense that people who have suffered brain trauma very much miss is the sense of smell. Not only is the sense of smell linked to taste, it also has powerful links to memory and emotions. Think of cordite in the air on Bonfire Night, the Christmas turkey roasting in the oven, the chemistry labs. Can you smell them right now?

It is possible in lessons to use the senses of smell and taste to increase concentration and aid memory. Try having indigenous plants and foods in the classroom when learning in geography about new countries, incense or myrrh in an RE lesson, or a couple of fresh baguettes in French. Chapter 5 gives more detail about additional visual and sensory supports for learning.

Verbal delivery

Have you listened to yourself when you are teaching? Very few teachers have recorded their lessons and really listened to themselves from a pupil's perspective. It is a fascinating exercise and very worthwhile. Teachers are good communicators. They have a lot to say and they say it well. But they say it fast. Teachers also move around and do other things as they speak; they turn to face the whiteboard, give out books or write a note. A slower verbal delivery actually helps both the teacher and the pupils. It gives the teacher time to think and choose words more carefully. It means pupils understand more of what is being said. Look at the pupils when speaking to the class so they can see your face, and use eye contact and gesture to enhance the meaning of what you say.

One question at a time

Asking questions is a vital part of teaching. Teachers ask questions to check understanding and knowledge, to develop pupils' thinking and to make lessons more interactive. Teachers often ask a question, and then immediately ask it again rephrased to aid understanding: but some pupils will have formulated the answer and have their hand up even before the teacher has finished asking the initial question.

Pupils with SEND need time to hear and process the question, search for the information they need for the answer, formulate a response, and then answer. This will take longer than you think. A slow count of ten is a useful length of time to allow for a considered response. If, while they are still thinking, the teacher rephrases the question and asks it again, the pupil will need to start the whole process again. In effect, they are being asked a new question before having had the chance to answer the previous one. This scenario makes pupils with SEND confused and sometimes distressed, and can frequently lead to challenging behaviour. One way to avoid this situation is to prepare the questions in advance for the pupil with SEND. The pupil could work on them at home, or in tutorial time, so that he or she will be prepared when the questions are asked in class. Alternatively, the pupil could work with the teaching assistant in the lesson to be ready to respond to a question in the plenary.

Use of language

Using simplified language does not mean that teachers need to 'talk down' to pupils with SEND. Again, problems often arise because teachers are such good communicators with wide vocabularies. When a pupil with SEND is in the class, try to say what you mean. English is ambiguous, full of inference, homonyms and synonyms. Be aware that a pupil is likely to misunderstand spoken information if they do not have additional cues, such as objects, pictures or signs.

Case study: Joe

Joe is in Year 7. In an October maths lesson Joe suddenly begins talking animatedly about ghosts and trick or treating. No matter how much his teacher asks him to be quiet he goes on talking about Hallowe'en. Eventually, he is sent out of the room. He is very distressed. At the end of the lesson the teacher asks Joe why he talked about Hallowe'en in the lesson. 'You asked me about it. You asked me about witches!' he replies. The teacher thinks back to the sentence she used before Joe had begun to speak. It was, 'Joe, *which is the larger amount?*'

Joe did not mean to behave badly. He thought he was answering his teacher's question. As it was the end of October it was not unreasonable for Joe to expect the teacher to talk about Hallowe'en, especially as he was going to a Hallowe'en party a few nights later.

Subject-specific vocabulary

Subject-specific vocabulary that has other meanings can cause comprehension problems. A way around this is to give pupils a dictionary (or glossary book) for each subject. The words they need to know can be written in the book with a simple explanation of the meaning in the context of that particular subject. For example, the word 'difference' may mean 'unlikeness' in common usage but, when asked to find the difference between two numbers, pupils need to know that in the context of a maths lesson it means subtraction of the smaller number from the larger. When asked to draw a table in maths, do not be surprised if what you get is what you sit at to eat your tea! In science, words such as 'conductor' and 'solution' need to have their meaning within the context explained carefully. This sort of work can be valuable preparation for starting new topics, and can be planned by the teaching assistant and/or given for homework. It can be a huge boost to self-esteem if a pupil with SEND can explain to the class at the beginning of a lesson the definition of a newly introduced word.

Choices

Everyone needs to be able to make sensible choices if they are to lead independent lives in adulthood. The reality for many pupils with SEND is that just about everything they do is directed by adults. Sadly, it is not uncommon to see pupils in Year 8 or 9 having their books opened for them and being handed a pen by a teaching assistant. It is interesting to have a member of staff monitor a pupil with SEND over one or two days, to log how many opportunities the pupil has to make choices. If children are deprived of choice they will give up trying to think for themselves, and become over-reliant on adults for all their needs. Build opportunities for choice into lessons, as basic as which pen to use, who to work with, where to sit, etc.

Individual subject targets

Short-term subject targets that are understood by and agreed with the pupil with SEND will provide a means of measuring progress over time. The targets may be linked to the pupil's individual learning targets, or may refer to skills and information specific to the subject. Make the targets visible by sticking them in the front of the exercise book or in the pupil's homework planner, and refer to them at the start and end of every lesson. The target needs to be worded in such a way that, when it is achieved, the pupil is able to say, 'Yes, I can do that'. For example, a target such as 'Solly will know six French words about the family: *maman, papa, soeur, frère, grandmère* and *grandpère*' is easy to record and assess; Solly understands what he has to learn and knows when he has achieved his target.

Recording

Thankfully, the days are long past when pupils spent hours each day copying down writing from the blackboard, although most recording in schools is still in writing, as are most of the ways that pupils show attainment. Nowadays, there are numerous alternatives to written methods that make recording more accessible and often more fun. Pupils making a video or audio diary can show greater understanding than in a written essay. Drawings or photo-montages often reveal great insight. Software packages, such as Clicker 6, give on-screen word banks and pictures that make writing less slow and arduous. Giving all pupils alternatives to writing can produce startling results, often the more so for pupils *without* SEND.

Children with all kinds of SEND will face problems in class with note taking or recording information. For many the problem will be the spelling or the required speed of writing. In most English lessons it will be necessary to work on written tasks, but in other subjects it is important to reflect on the purpose and necessity for the writing. The usual reason for note taking is to enable pupils to access information from the lesson for homework and future examinations. As long as that information is available, the format is not and should not be important. A simple summary or aide-memoire can be prepared by the TA for example, and clipped into the pupil's folder, with a sentence or two added by the pupil, possibly dictated to the TA where time is limited.

Pupils with more significant SEND will need to be offered alternatives to writing in order to record information for later revision. By accepting a range of methods of recording, teachers will be liberating pupils with SEND from the tyranny of the pen. Some pupils with SEND may think of a wonderful sentence but will have forgotten it by the time they have finished writing the first word. That doesn't mean that teachers should give up on developing pupils' writing ability, but there is little point in them simply copying an adult's writing that they do not understand, and cannot read back. Here are some ideas for alternative ways of recording.

Photographs

For pupils with SEND, a cheap camera or old phone will revolutionise recording. Let them photograph the sequence of activities in practical tasks, or allow them as a means later of recording and remembering that activity to sequence a series of photographs of, for example, a science experiment.

Computers

Laptop or tablet computers with symbol software or Clicker 6 (Crick Software) grids give pupils with SEND an independent way of recording what they have learned. Clicker 6 grids for a wide range of subjects are available on the Internet at www.LearningGrids.com. Most of the grids have been designed by teachers who put them on the website for others to use.

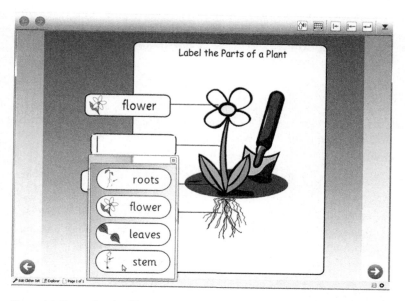

Figure 4.6 Example of a Clicker 6 grid (reproduced by permission of Crick Software, www.cricksoft.com)

Drawings

Some pupils with SEND prefer to draw a picture as a way of remembering what they have learned. They need to be able to look at pictures at a future date and understand the meaning behind them. Asking the pupil to tell an adult about a picture and describe exactly what they say; this will tell you how much the pupil has understood and learned.

Video and audio recordings

Recording lessons on audio files (or on video if you're feeling brave) gives pupils the option to listen to or watch the lesson again at home. Where the purpose of note taking and recording is to give pupils information to revise for future examinations, audio or video recordings will serve that same purpose in a more accessible format. Allowing pupils to record their own interpretation of the key lesson objectives in an audio or video file quickly builds up a bank of resources that can be used both for recording and for assessment. Teach the pupil to speak each sentence into an old Dictaphone, and then rewind and listen as they write; this frees them from the need for one-to-one support.

Sequencing

'Death by Worksheets' is a common feature of school for pupils with SEND. Worksheets are useful for differentiating work for different abilities in the class, and where the worksheets are well designed most pupils enjoy completing them. A useful way of developing skills through worksheets for pupils with SEND is to design the worksheets as a cut-and-stick sequencing activity. Pictures and corresponding sentences can be mixed up on the worksheet. The pupil cuts them out and sequences the pictures in the right order and then matches the sentences. No matter what the subject, this approach works well. The pupil does not need to write, and the activity involves fine motor skills, reading, and if organised as a paired or group activity, speaking and listening.

Cloze procedure

Simple cloze procedure worksheets are useful for pupils who can read, but who find writing and spelling difficult. These worksheets can easily be differentiated with the missing words and symbol supports at the bottom or at the side of the page.

Scribing

Scribing is a valuable technique to use when teachers really want a pupil's ideas and creativity to shine through. Pupils can either speak directly to another pupil or an adult, or they can record on an audio file. Structure the scribing with questions, pictures or objects, and this will avoid the pupil losing the thread of what they want to say. In an English lesson on poetry, give a pupil with SEND an object to hold – an orange perhaps. Let the pupil feel it and write down the words they use – smooth, round. Peel it – soft, furry. Smell it – fresh, fruity, tangy. Taste it – sharp, sweet, juicy. Put the words together and you have the basis of a poem.

Modern foreign languages

In many schools pupils with SEND are disapplied from modern foreign languages, with the time so released often used for tutorials and extra work on basic literacy and numeracy

Alternatives to writing for recording and presenting information

Photographs

Concept maps

Voice to text software

On-screen word banks (Clicker 6, Communicate: In Print 2)

Drawings or pictures

Symbols

Audio files

Video

PowerPoint presentation

Sequencing pictures or word cards

Cut and stick worksheets

Cloze text – filling in missing words

Figure 4.7 Alternatives to writing

skills. This is in many ways unfortunate, as learning a new language is the one area where pupils start from an equal basis. Pupils with SEND do not bring to this new subject the memories of past failures and can be very motivated to learn. Teaching in modern foreign language lessons is also usually very lively and interactive, with many opportunities for active learning – and the promise of trips abroad in the future. Learning about different cultures and environments and even a few foreign words can enhance children's self-esteem and give them a real sense of 'belonging' within a mainstream peer group.

Assessment

Measure what you value rather than value what you can measure. Repetition of this saying is not a mistake. For pupils with SEND it is a necessity. For some pupils what might seem like an everyday achievement, such as being able to use public transport independently, is as important an achievement as is gaining five grade A to Cs at GCSE for their peers. This book recommends setting a few precise targets in all subjects for pupils with SEND. Precise targets are easier to assess and having only two or three targets limits the paperwork.

Where targets are based on P scales or National Curriculum programmes of study, pupils can be assessed against national benchmarks. These give schools the information they need to show the value-added for a particular pupil. It is useful to have across the curriculum a system of observations for pupils with SEND which identifies successful strategies and gains impartial insights into pupils' learning and behaviour. The observations feed into the assessment process, and so into planning for future inclusion. A form for recording these observations follows.

Name of pupil _____ Class/Year group _____

Date:	Observer:	Subject:

Pupil responses to ...

Teaching strategies

Support

Behaviour management

Resources

Date:	Observer:	Subject:

Pupil responses to ...

Teaching strategies

Support

Behaviour management

Resources

Date:	Observer:	Subject:

Pupil responses to ...

Teaching strategies

Support

Behaviour management

Resources

Notes:

Figure 4.8 Template for observation recording form

The most effective way of recording achievement for pupils with SEND is by using progress files. A section for each subject can be filled with pieces of work, photographs and reports. A new file for each school year will build up a valuable record of the pupil's achievements and experiences over time.

Summary

The bases for successful inclusion in secondary schools are:

- *Planning*: tracking back, key concepts or curriculum overlapping, make it possible to plan to include a pupil with SEND as part of the planning for the rest of the class.
- *Teamwork*: with other teachers, the SENCO, teaching assistants and other professionals.
- *Flexibility*: accept different ways of recording and different ways of communicating.
- *Links*: make links between subjects explicit and visual.
- *Supports*: look beyond teaching assistants to peer support, visual and other sensory supports, and information technology.

Chapter 5 looks at support for inclusion in more detail.

Chapter 5

Support for inclusion

What is learning support?

The term 'learning support' covers all those activities which enable a school to respond to the diverse range of needs and abilities of pupils. Learning support is about more than pupils with SEND; it is a whole-school issue aimed at supporting the development of more inclusive systems in the school, rather than merely helping individual pupils. If support is to be wholly effective it must be founded on respect for all pupils, including pupils with SEND, and those pupils' right to be full members of the school community.

Learning support is exactly what it says on the tin – support to help pupils learn more effectively. Support for learning comes in many different forms, shapes and sizes, and to be most effective needs to permeate all areas of school life.

Support for learning will come from:

*   adults, including specialist teachers, teaching assistants, parents, and volunteers;
*   other pupils;
*   a range of teaching strategies and styles;
*   visual and other sensory supports;
*   information technology;
*   resources;
*   outside agencies such as local authority teams or voluntary groups.

> Support that is clearly defined, structured and consistent makes the difference between a successful long-term placement and one that ends in failure.

Developing learning support for inclusion

Among both teachers and support staff there are often fundamental misunderstandings about inclusion and what inclusion really means. Developing a shared vision of inclusion is the first step to improving the quality and effectiveness of support for learning.

People ask:

'How can it be inclusion if one pupil gets much more than another?'

and say:

'There are lots of pupils who would attain much more if they had support from a teaching assistant.'

or:

'It isn't fair that pupils with SEND have support from teaching assistants while others don't.'

or:

'Inclusion means all pupils doing the same thing.'

Everyone involved with pupils who have SEND need to understand the school's inclusive values and ethos, and to subscribe to that in both policy and practice. Appropriate training helps to shape attitudes and will ensure that everyone is 'singing from the same hymn sheet'. The training activities below are a useful way to start discussion and to develop understanding about inclusion. They are suitable for use with school staff, governors and parents.

Training activity 1   Inclusion – definitions

Organisation: whole group together with one person recording what is said on a flipchart.

Resources:

*   paper and pens;
*   box;
*   flipchart.

1   Each person writes a brief definition of inclusion.
2   The definitions are folded and placed in a box.
3   The box is shaken and everyone takes out a definition.
4   This definition is shared with one other person and key words noted – e.g. all, welcome, etc.
5   Write the key words on a flipchart.
6   As a group, use the key words to write a definition of inclusion with which all can agree.

Training activity 2 The 'no buts' zone

Organisation: all together, seated in a circle.

Resources: one red chair – the 'hot seat'.

The group moves around the circle, from one chair to the next. The person sitting in the 'hot seat' says something positive about including pupils who have SEND, or they move on to the next chair without comment. A previously used comment may be repeated. The only rule is that no one is allowed to say 'but'.

This is a very simple yet powerful activity. Hearing the positive benefits of inclusion without the negatives – the 'buts' – begins to change perceptions and attitudes.

Training activity 3 On the cards

Organisation: groups of four people.

Resources:

- One envelope for each group.
- Each envelope contains one card with the integration definition below, one card with the inclusion definition and two blank cards.

1   In the groups, open the envelope and set out the cards with the integration card on the left, the inclusion card on the right, and the two blank cards in between.
2   Discuss the definitions.
3   On each of the blank cards, write down an action a school could take to move from the integration model to inclusion as defined on the cards.
4   As a plenary, write up all actions on a flipchart and discuss with the whole group.

Integration	Inclusion
A process by which individual children are supported in order that they can participate in the existing (and largely unchanged) programme of the school.	A willingness to restructure the school's programme in response to the diversity of the pupils who attend.

Figure 5.1 Inclusion definition activity cards

Inclusion does not mean that everyone should receive the same provision, nor does it mean that all pupils should fit into the same systems in school. It is up to schools to adapt their systems to meet the needs of a diverse group of pupils and to ensure that every pupil receives the provision that he or she needs. In *inclusive* schools, each child is given the level of provision and support they need, and receives it regardless of ability.

In mainstream schools, all too often the reality for pupils with SEND is that they spend most lessons sitting next to an adult and speaking mostly to adults. It is sad to see a pupil with SEND working hard for every minute of the lesson with an adult making sure that he or she stays on task. Look around the class – you will see other pupils chatting quietly, gazing out of the window or just daydreaming. Very few pupils work consistently throughout lessons, yet often this is what is expected of pupils with SEND. They probably work harder than the majority of their classmates.

Teaching assistants and other adults

Over the past twenty years there has been a significant growth in the number of teaching assistants in secondary schools. The support given by teaching assistants to groups or individual pupils can improve access to the curriculum, raise self-esteem, encourage positive behaviour, and so have a beneficial effect for all. The challenge is that there is very little research evidence to show this positive impact. Indeed, the Deployment and Impact of Support Staff (DISS) research project (Blatchford *et al.*, 2009) from the Institute of Education found that teaching assistants made either no impact or had a negative impact on the progress of pupils with SEND. Blatchford *et al.* make the point that 'there has been an ad hoc drift toward a kind of deployment of TAs that, while conducted with the best of intentions, has resulted in unintended and unacceptable consequences (2012, p. 8). This doesn't mean that teaching assistants cannot have a positive impact on the progress of pupils with SEND, or that they are failing in their work. Rather, the failure lies in their deployment and management, especially their role in supporting pupils with SEND – the most vulnerable pupils in our schools who need access to the best and the most skilled teaching.

The DISS research was presaged by the Ofsted report 'Inclusion: does it matter where pupils are taught? Provision and outcomes in different settings for pupils with SEND and disabilities' (Ofsted, 2006) which found that 'Pupils in mainstream schools where support from teaching assistants was the main type of provision were less likely to make good academic progress than those who had access to specialist teaching in those schools' (p. 3).

In *Maximising the Impact of Teaching Assistants*, Russell *et al.* (2013, p. 14) suggest three main explanations for the findings of the DISS project:

1   TAs have a mainly pedagogical role and work most often with lower-attaining pupils with the danger that these pupils can become distanced from the teacher and the curriculum.
2   The limited time and opportunities that teachers and teaching assistants have to plan together and discuss pupils' learning needs.
3   The interactions between teaching assistants and pupils are less demanding and focus on pupils' completing tasks rather than on their learning from those tasks.

Compounding this situation is the lack of training given to teachers on how effectively to manage other adults in lessons, and the fact that training on SEND in schools is most often accessed by teaching assistants rather than teachers. Michael Giangreco (2003, p. 51) calls this the 'training trap'– where the well-intended training of teaching assistants can inadvertently lead to teachers increasingly relinquishing responsibility for pupils with SEND to those assistants. This was brought home in one school where the headteacher proudly shared a booklet written by a teaching assistant following some in-service training on working with pupils with Autistic Spectrum Disorder. The cover of the booklet showed a picture of ET and had the title, 'An alien in our school'. Clearly, the teaching assistant had seen Clare Sainsbury's book *Martian in the Playground: Understanding the Schoolchild with Asperger's Syndrome* (2010) but had failed to understand the insensitivity of describing a child with ASD as an alien.

In the 2006 report, Ofsted identifies two actions that schools should take to improve the deployment and impact of teaching assistants. These are:

- analyse critically the use and deployment of teaching assistants:

    - Schools need to know the impact of their teaching assistants and other support staff on both the academic progress and well-being of all pupils, including those with SEND. This is especially critical now that SEND budgets are delegated to schools who will need to account both for how that SEND budget has been used and what benefits that budget has produced for pupils with SEND.

- increase the amount of specialist teaching provided for a range of SEND within a broad and balanced curriculum, developing knowledge and skills relating to SEND across the school workforce (p. 5):

    - Although specialist teachers may cost more than teaching assistants, often they have a greater impact on the progress of pupils with SEND. Training on all aspects of SEND should be accessed by all staff so that the quality of teaching is improved and teachers feel more confident to work closely with pupils with SEND and to manage any additional adults in the classroom.

It is vital that teaching assistants are involved in lesson planning so that they understand the aims of the lessons and are aware of the teachers' expectations of their role in that context. This is equally necessary for teaching assistants assigned to faculties as it is for those whose identified role is to support an individual pupil with SEND.

The ideal situation is for the pupil who has SEND to develop good working relationships with all the adults in the classroom, including volunteers and students. This can be achieved by scheduling all adults to support the pupil over the course of a week. This variety of support will also give different perspectives on the pupil's progress and attainment that will inform assessments, target setting and reports.

Teaching assistants should always be deployed in ways that foster the independence of pupils, and which enable them to be full and valued members of the class. In effect, the most successful teaching assistants are working themselves out of a job! The day when a pupil no longer needs individual TA support ought to be a day of celebration.

Individual support

Some pupils with more significant SEND are likely to have a number of support hours allocated through an EHC plan. These hours can often cover most of the time the pupil is in school. The close relationship that develops between pupils with SEND and the teaching assistant who usually supports them can be positive when the support is sensitive, and helps the pupil to be a full member of the class. Equally, if the teaching assistant's role and the desired outcomes for the pupil are not made clear, the situation can become oppressive for both parties where they are expected to work together for long periods of time.

When a pupil has additional behavioural difficulties, the teaching assistant is often the only person who knows the pupil well enough to encourage him/her to stay on task, and too often is the only person dealing directly with the inappropriate behaviours. This situation causes intolerable stress and cannot be maintained in the long term.

Where a pupil has a high number of teaching assistant hours, it is always best to share those hours between at least two teaching assistants, so that if one person is ill another can provide cover. It also helps to prevent the pupil from becoming dependent on one particular teaching assistant. Ideas, strategies and tasks can also be shared during 'overlap' periods when both adults are in school and can meet together with the teacher.

Support hours detailed on EHC plans need not tie one particular teaching assistant to a pupil for the amount of time specified. Schools are free to deploy teaching assistants to the best advantage of the pupils in a particular situation. Try adjusting working times for one or two days each week, so that teaching assistants arrive before the start of school, or stay after the end of the school day. These measures create opportunities for teaching assistants to:

- talk to other teaching assistants;
- support the teachers to plan and differentiate learning activities and tasks;
- prepare resources;
- share training;
- attend staff meetings;
- contribute to assessments and reports.

All these activities provide support just as much as having the teaching assistant seated next to the pupil. Involving teaching assistants in planning, and ensuring they have plenty of positive feedback about their work, gives them the professional status they deserve.

Support at breaks and lunchtime

Some pupils have support hours detailed for the unstructured time in school, such as lunchtime and breaks. Where a teaching assistant supports a pupil at breaktimes, avoid the teaching assistant taking on the role of 'minder'. Their most effective role is that of distant observer: close enough to intervene if necessary, but at a distance that allows the student to interact independently with others. This is a valuable opportunity for formal and informal observations of a pupil's social skills, and for identifying areas for development.

It is imperative that training is made available before another adult, such as a lunch-time supervisor, takes on responsibility for supporting a pupil with SEND. This is not

Support for independence

- knowing when to stand back and encourage pupil to make own decisions
- expecting pupil to work unsupported for part of each lesson
- developing independence in physical needs, such as using the toilet

Social interaction

- supporting pupil as member of a collaborative group
- promoting peer acceptance
- helping pupil develop social and organisational skills
- organising games to include the child with SEND

Professional liaison

- working alongside teachers to plan curriculum access and set targets
- delivering programmes devised to meet specific needs
- observing and recording pupil responses
- monitoring behaviour, e.g. time spent on task
- releasing the teacher so s/he can work with small groups
- liaising with other professionals
- contributing to annual and SEN reviews
- preparing appropriate resources

Figure 5.2 What support might look like

a situation where a willing mum can be drafted in at short notice. There must also be daily communication with the form tutor or SENCO and teaching assistants so that the supervisor is aware of any important information regarding the pupil, such as, for example, any changes in behaviour strategies.

Support towards independence

All pupils need to develop individual and group working skills if they are to become more independent as they grow. Stand back and allow pupils to make their own decisions – this is a vital part of support for learning. Even when support is needed with personal care, pupils should be encouraged to be responsible for as much of their own care as possible. It is very difficult to wean pupils off individual support once they have become dependent, so they need to get used to working without support for part of every lesson, if at first for only five minutes. For this to be possible teachers will need to devise activities that can be completed without constant support. Activities such as small group games, matching and sorting activities linked to the subject area, listening to an audio book, etc., are easy to prepare and have a definite finish. To release teaching assistants from supporting one pupil all the time also frees them to work with other pupils and gives more variety to their work.

Social interaction

Wherever possible, encourage a pupil to work as part of a collaborative group, even if he or she already has one-to-one support. Social interaction is enhanced when pupils work together – for instance, in a jigsaw-structure activity. Other pupils are often unsure how to speak with and behave towards a pupil with SEND, and a teaching assistant can be a valuable role model for positive and equal interactions.

Personal organisation

Pupils with SEND often find it very difficult to organise their belongings. Wherever possible, remind pupils verbally and in writing about any equipment they will need for the next lesson or of changes to the schedule. Where a pupil has particular difficulties remembering what to bring, give him or her a picture list of the equipment needed for a particular activity or lesson, e.g. swimming or PE kit. Visual reminders such as small cards attached to a key ring showing equipment, or a timetable, will develop confidence and independence for individual pupils. With these strategies pupils with SEND gradually develop that sense of responsibility they will need when they go to college or start work.

Professional liaison

Teaching assistants who support individual pupils with SEND need to have time other than in lessons to talk to the SENCO and subject teachers. This liaison must be timetabled and given a high priority by leadership teams if it is not to be undermined by other imperatives. By discussing the pupil's progress together, the SENCO, teachers and teaching assistants can ensure access for individual pupils and effectively incorporate learning objectives into lessons. Without this liaison, teaching assistants have to work in isolation, and may need to adapt inappropriate activities and resources while a lesson is actually taking place.

Often teaching assistants will notice incidents in lessons missed by teachers because of the teacher's necessary focus on the whole class, but may have no time to pass this information on at the end of the lesson. A concise form is a useful way of transferring information that can be used as part of the assessment process and which will inform the planning of future lessons.

Comments written by teaching assistants should be predominantly positive. Try to start out by noting what the pupil has done well and then comment on areas of difficulty. For example:

A form that can be used by teaching assistants to record pupil responses follows on p. 96 (Figure 5.3).

Case study: Khalid

Extract from Khalid's Maths support liaison form

Year 7 Maths: Shape and Space: 3-D shapes

Khalid sat quietly and listened to the first part of the lesson. He tried hard in the group activity and correctly named the cube and cuboid. Khalid had difficulty understanding the individual task. He became distressed and refused to attempt the work. When calm, he worked on a construction kit from his maths activity box. He created several 3-D shapes. Khalid took photos of his finished shapes and stuck them in his maths folder.

Written information about a lesson such as this gives a firm basis for assessing Khalid's level of understanding and informs future lesson planning. It does not duck the issue of Khalid's inappropriate behaviour. It puts into context a task he did not understand and shows how the difficulties were resolved.

Multidisciplinary teams

Teaching assistants are a vital part of the multidisciplinary team involved with a pupil with SEND, and close liaison with other professionals and parents will be necessary. This is especially the case if the teaching assistant is to work with the pupil on, for example, a motor skills programme under the direction of an occupational therapist. Where therapy targets, or targets based on advice from other outside professionals are worked on in school, a much more joined-up and holistic approach to meeting the pupil's needs can be developed. If these targets are incorporated as far as possible into planning for learning activities, the need for withdrawal from lessons can be minimised. Remember, by withdrawing a pupil for therapy he or she misses some part of the curriculum in class. Achieving a balance between therapy and curriculum imperatives can be difficult and will depend on the individual needs of the pupil. Discuss this balance with therapists – this often leads to a creative solution and a plan for an effective series of lessons.

Other adults

Other adults in school – parents and grandparents, volunteers, student teachers, governors – are a really valuable resource and an ideal way to vary the support for pupils who have SEND. This less formal support helps pupils develop social and interaction skills with a wider range of people. These new people bring fresh perspectives and expectations, even new topics of conversation, to expand a pupil's vocabulary.

Wider contacts with additional adults also serve to reassure other parents about what they may think are the effects of the pupil with SEND learning alongside their own children. Some parents may be anxious, for instance, that the teacher might spend too long with the child with special educational needs at the expense of the rest of the class. The more people know about how an inclusive classroom works, the better they will appreciate the benefits for all pupils.

Pupil: _____   Class/Year group: _____   Supported by: _____

Date	Subject/objectives	Pupil responses	Comments

Figure 5.3 Template for TA recording and feedback form

Peer support

Peer support for pupils with SEND is an effective and powerful tool for inclusion; yet schools often are remarkably reluctant to make use of this natural resource. There is a frequent fear that parents of the supporting pupils will object, that it is unfair on the other students, or that work will suffer as a consequence. Peer support in practice is rarely a burden for pupils and is usually of benefit to all concerned. Buddy systems and Circles of Friends are powerful ways to include pupils who need a little help to become part of the school community.

Buddies

It is reasonable to expect one pupil to help another from time to time. A buddy system simply makes that help more formal and gives the supporters a framework within which to operate. The majority of buddy systems are based on pairing pupils in order, for example, to guide and support a new pupil through the initial settling-in process. Such a paired system could put too much responsibility on one child, so for pupils who have SEND, a buddy scheme involving a small number of supporters – four or five – is more appropriate.

Careful selection of buddies at the outset is important for the future success of the scheme. Buddies can be chosen either from the pupil's own class or from an older year group, depending on whether the support is for all the time in school, or only for breaks and lunchtimes. If the support is to be effective, preparation for the buddies is very important, with the boundaries of their role carefully defined. For example, the buddy's role in the playground might be to talk with the pupil with SEND and encourage him or her to join games or interact with others. The buddy would not be expected to intervene in disputes with other pupils, except to inform a member of staff. The amount of time spent in support should be limited, and buddies need to have time to give feedback to staff. There also needs to be time to discuss any issues that may arise. A written schedule of regular support and feedback meetings will protect all the parties from becoming overburdened.

Case study: David

David has problems during transition between classes. He is frequently accused of assaulting other pupils and he regularly runs out of school. David is in Year 7 and he has an Autistic Spectrum Disorder and moderate learning difficulties. He thinks he is being attacked by other students when they touch him with their elbows or their bags in the busy corridors. His response is to hit out and try to get away as quickly as possible. David is well behaved in class and in his primary school he had no behaviour difficulties. The behaviour support service teacher recommended a buddy scheme involving four boys from David's form group. The boys were asked to walk with David between lessons, one at each side of him, one in front and one behind. In this way David is shielded from other pupils and cannot be knocked by them. In conjunction with the buddy scheme, a narrative was written to explain to David that the collisions in the corridor were not meant as attacks. The narrative teaches him alternative ways of behaving when he feels anxious.

After two weeks David no longer needed the formal support of his buddies and they were able to walk with him in a more natural grouping. All four boys were glad to help David and, as they came to know him better, they began to like him and to want to spend time with him, especially when they found out about his expertise on computer games.

Talk partners

The talk partner system commonly used in primary schools can also be used successfully in secondary schools as an effective way of supporting less confident pupils. Talk partners support pupils with SEND very well, enable them to answer questions and encourage speaking and listening. Sometimes teaching assistants act as a talk partner for the pupil they support, but it is more effective if the pupil has another student acting as the partner, possibly with the teaching assistant supporting them both.

Circle of Friends

The Circle of Friends approach originated in North America and has been used in mainstream settings to support pupils with a wide range of SEN and disabilities. The circle consists of between six and eight pupils who volunteer to form a support network for a particular student. The Circle of Friends is led by an adult, usually an educational psychologist or a teacher. A weekly meeting with the whole circle is held to discuss any difficulties and to work out ways of resolving problems for the pupil.

The Circle of Friends has three main aims:

- to create for the student with SEND a support network of other pupils;
- to provide the pupil with encouragement and recognition for achievements and progress;
- to work with the pupil to identify difficulties, and to come up with practical ideas to help sort out problems.

Setting up a circle includes:

- gaining the support and agreement of the focus pupil and his or her parents;
- a meeting with the whole class (which the focus pupil does not attend) aimed at identifying those willing to be supporters;
- informing the parents of those chosen to be circle members and gaining their agreement to their son or daughter's participation;
- weekly meetings of the circle, the focus pupil and an adult facilitator.

(Newton and Wilson, 2003)

The time commitment of the circle members needs to be monitored carefully to make sure the support is not taking up too much of their time and is being shared equally among the group. The time commitment for staff is roughly 40–60 minutes to set up the circle, with weekly meetings each lasting 20–30 minutes. A bonus of the Circle of Friends approach is that where some of the circle members themselves have emotional or social difficulties, the circle often has a positive effect on their behaviour and self-esteem in school, in addition to the positive support for the focus student.

Medication

When planning to include pupils with SEND, an issue that causes schools much anxiety is the administration of medicines. Medication may need to be administered regularly (an inhaler for asthma) or perhaps only in an emergency situation (following an epileptic seizure). Many pupils at some time need to take medicines in school, whether antibiotics for an infection or an antihistamine for hay fever, and training is needed to know how and when to administer various drugs – and good quality training is the key to raising staff confidence. As many adults as possible need to be trained to be sure that someone is available at all times.

Other sensory supports

The day-to-day delivery of the secondary school curriculum relies on pupils being able to hear, understand, read and write at an appropriate level. Where pupils are unable to meet these criteria, other ways of delivering the curriculum need to be found, but experience has taught us that additional sensory supports will help all the class, not merely those pupils with SEND.

Visual supports

Visual supports include objects, photographs, drawings, symbols, signing, text and moving images. Never underestimate the power of pictures or objects. Film is an important medium because it is so visual. Silent movies can deliver just as powerful a message as films with sound – sometimes even more so.

Visual languages such as symbols and signing support the development of reading and writing and aid communication.

Symbols

We are surrounded by symbols in everyday life – from road signs to the symbol above the fast-food restaurant. Using symbols to support language and literacy builds on this natural pictorial communication. Symbols act as a bridge for pupils who have difficulties with literacy. It helps to sequence words and ideas, and frees intellectual development from the constraints of reading and writing. In text, pictographic cues help pupils begin the decoding and encoding process. Symbols differ from text in that each concept is represented by one image rather than a group of phonemes. For example:

Figure 5.4 Cat symbol

There are many words that have more than one meaning. By using symbols the intended meaning can be accurately represented. For example:

saw   saw   saw

Figure 5.5

Symbols:

- are internationally recognised;
- overcome language barriers;
- are pictorial or abstract;
- communicate ideas quickly and simply.

Symbolic development

While many symbols are iconic and easily recognisable, others are abstract. Pupils need to learn an abstract symbol in real contexts. As an instance, the symbol for 'dog' is a picture of a dog. Most children have experienced dogs in many different situations and their understanding of the concept 'dog' enables them to understand the symbol. The symbol for 'over', however, is abstract, and the pupil would need to learn the meaning of this symbol in real situations. The symbol for 'over' might be introduced when the pupil is climbing over a bench or putting a cloth over a bowl. When introducing new concepts, always teach the pupil a symbol in context.

The understanding of symbols is hierarchical. Children need to understand a symbol in more than one manifestation before their understanding can be assumed. The progression for symbolic development is as follows:

- real objects;
- representative objects;
- photographs;
- coloured pictures/drawings and line drawings;
- standardised symbol systems;
- written words.

Real objects

Real objects exist in three dimensions. They can be touched, held and turned. They have form, size and textures. They may have taste and smell. Children at early stages of development need to have the symbol or sign introduced at the same time as they experience the object.

Objects are a powerful tool for supporting speech and text. Sensory boxes linked to texts in English bring the words to life. Pupils who find reading challenging can access the texts through film, audio files, pictures and objects together. Thus, they are enabled to give their interpretation of the text because they have had support for their understanding.

Box 5.1 A sensory box for Macbeth

You will need:

- a copy of the text;
- a piece of tartan cloth;
- a plastic cauldron containing toy mice, frog, insects, etc.;
- a wooden spoon;
- three witches' hats;
- a cardboard crown;
- a plastic knife;
- a rubber glove dipped in red paint;
- photographs of castles;
- leafy branches;
- audio file of bagpipe music.

witch

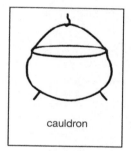
cauldron

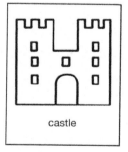
castle

king

Figure 5.6 Symbols from Macbeth

Representative objects

Representative objects are the next level of symbolic development. These are usually miniature objects – for instance, a small plastic animal or a toy vacuum cleaner. The pupil needs to understand that the small or toy object represents something real – for example, that a small plastic dog represents a real dog.

Photographs

Usually, photographs are the first two-dimensional representation presented to children. The change from 3-D to 2-D can pose real perceptual difficulties for some pupils, and at first photographs need to be presented in conjunction with either the real object or a representative object.

Photographs should be used with caution because they can be very confusing. Pupils with SEND are often given photographic timetables in school. Problems arise when photographs in the timetable are of the focus pupil working in different classrooms (one photograph looks very much like another). Where photographs contain too much visual information, pupils will not be able to differentiate what is important and what is not. If photographs are used, they need to be of one object or of one person, on a plain background. Any more information will confuse pupils. For example:

Julio has an Autistic Spectrum Disorder. His visual timetable is made up of photographs, one of which is of the minibus that brings him to school. Every time Julio sees the photograph he says, 'baa'. No one can understand why he says this, nor will he say 'bus' or 'home' when he sees the photo. After several weeks, a teaching assistant notices a speck in the corner of the photo. Under a magnifying glass the speck is found to be a sheep in the distance. She cuts around the minibus in the photo and mounts it on card. Soon Julio is saying 'bus' when shown the picture of the minibus.

Coloured pictures/drawings and line drawings

If pupils are to use symbols and signs successfully, the ability to understand that a drawing represents a real object or situation is necessary. The drawings need to be clear and simple, with little or no background detail. If a pupil has experienced either a real dog or a toy dog, they will know that a dog has four legs, two ears, two eyes and a tail. A drawing of a dog may show the dog sitting down or in profile. The pupil has to take his or her

Figure 5.7 Dog illustration

knowledge of a dog – four legs, two ears, etc. – and translate that knowledge into the two-dimensional image of the picture above. This picture shows only two obvious legs, and neither a tail nor any ears or eyes. For adults this is obviously a dog, but this will be much less clear to pupils with learning difficulties. Such a picture would need to be introduced alongside representative objects or photographs.

Standardised symbol systems

Standardised symbols are the first clear link with reading. Just as a word has to represent a whole genus, so does a symbol. For example, a pupil may have a pet German Shepherd dog at home; a photograph can show an individual poodle, but the symbol has to represent all dogs, from Great Danes to a Jack Russell. Understanding this shift is an important developmental milestone.

There are a number of symbol systems that are used in schools. It does not matter which system is used, but it is important to decide on one, and stick to it to avoid confusion. Communicate in Print 2 software from Widgit has several symbol systems available that can be easily created by simply typing in the words. To support communication, the symbols can then be used in grids or to support text.

Written words

Understanding of the written word is the goal for all pupils. Symbols support reading development by giving visual cues above or below the words and can help to develop left to right tracking. Colour coding the symbols gives pupils an understanding of sentence structure.

Respiration symbols

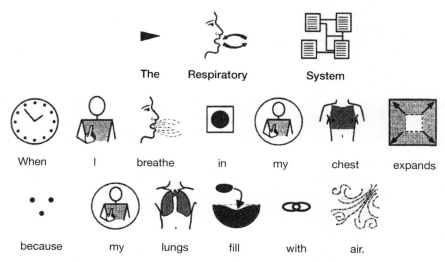

Figure 5.8 Respiration symbols

The following are some ideas on how to use symbols to support individuals and groups of pupils.

Visual timetables

Visual timetables (see Figure 5.9) are easy to make and give vital support to pupils with SEND. Symbols may be added to the usual school timetable or the symbols can be mounted on to card and fixed to a board with hook and loop tape. This has the advantage of being easy to alter should any changes occur, such as for the Christmas concert or a visiting theatre group.

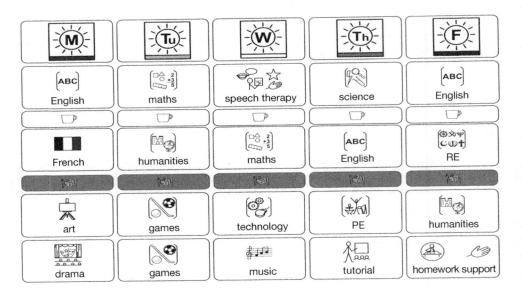

Figure 5.9 Symbols timetable

Communication boards

Communication boards are valuable tools in the classroom. They are unobtrusive but very effective. The boards are organised in a grid format that contains the pupil's most commonly used symbols. These can be general symbols such as 'toilet', 'drink', 'hurt', 'yes' and 'no', etc., as well as symbols for different subjects and/or photographs of key people. Bear in mind that it is important to teach symbols *before* they are added to a communication board. If the board is kept on the desk, the pupil, teacher or teaching assistant can point to the relevant symbol or photograph to support understanding.

Communication books

A cheap A5 photograph album is ideal for this purpose. The pages hold a selection of small symbol cards, and a strip of hook and loop tape on the front cover holds the pupil's chosen symbol sequence. The book also can be used by the adults working with the pupil to support understanding, and to let the pupil know what is to happen next.

Figure 5.10 Communication board

Access to information

As students move towards adulthood they need access to a wide range of important information that is usually text based: safety information, manuals for electrical equipment, recipes, menus, games instructions. All this vital information is easily translated into symbols using Communicate in Print 2 software. Information on sexual health, or the instructions on how to use a fire extinguisher, may even save a life. Symbol access to this information gives a measure of independence and develops self-advocacy, and enables people to make their own life choices.

Other symbol supports for communication

Some pupils are very reluctant to use large communication boards or books outside the classroom. Adolescent pupils do not want to appear different, so need a more subtle approach. A small personal organiser will hold sufficient symbol cards to support communication between students in the canteen or on the school bus. For students who need only a few symbols, laminate the cards and attach them to a key ring. This will give easy access in less formal situations.

Memory mats

Memory mats are a valuable resource for pupils who need visual reminders to help them remember commonly used information. The mat is made of a piece of A3 card with space for a book marked out in the centre. Around the edge of the mat are written the letters of the alphabet, important subject-specific vocabulary, days of the week and months of the year, numbers and number words to 20 – any information that will support the pupil and aid independent working. The mats will last for a long time if they are laminated.

The pupil may either have one mat that is kept in his or her bag, or a different mat can be created for each subject.

1 2 3 4 5 6 7 8 9 10 11 12 13 14 15 16 17 18 19 20		

one
two
three
four
five
six
seven
eight
nine
ten
		+ add
		
		− take away
		   subtract
		
		× times
		
		= equals
		   same as

a b c d e f g h i j k l m n o p q r s t u v w x y z		

Figure 5.11 An example of a memory mat

Signing

Just as symbols are all around us, so all of us use signing to some extent, but we call it gesture. We point, we touch and we wave our arms around. Many people find it impossible to communicate without using their hands. Gesture is a means of adding nuance to speech and it helps listeners to understand.

Less than 10 per cent of our understanding of language comes from the words we hear. The remainder of our understanding comes from the context, facial expression, body language, tone of voice and gesture. Children with SEND often have difficulty understanding and using the full range of communicative skills. They may be able to use facial expression, but might not be able to understand the minute sophisticated changes between a smile and a sneer – a small facial movement that makes a huge difference to the meaning.

Signing supports communication both by giving pupils with SEND a visual support for understanding speech and by enabling them to make themselves better understood. Signing provides the means for them to let others know what they think about life in general and school in particular. Impaired communication further excludes pupils with SEND from other areas of school life, such as clubs and social events. Signing provides support to help pupils relax with each other and share experiences. Teaching all the school to sign one or two songs for the Christmas carol service will boost both the self-esteem of pupils with SEND and the signing skills of the whole community. As part of the concert, teach the congregation the signs for the chorus of one of the carols – it's quite a moving sight to see a large group of people signing together.

Parents are sometimes concerned that their child will stop trying to speak if they are taught to sign, but the opposite is the case. Signing both supports and encourages children to speak, and signs are only ever used in addition to speech. As with symbols, pupils gradually build up a vocabulary of signs, and start with commonly used words, such as mum, good, hello, book, etc. Again, as with symbols, signs must be taught with real objects or in real situations if pupils are to attach the correct meaning to the sign.

If signing is to be effective and useful, other people in school need to be able to sign at the same level as the pupils with SEND. This will involve training for parents, teachers, teaching assistants and other pupils. An ideal way of introducing signing is to teach the whole school community. Regular signing assemblies, and after-school or lunchtime signing clubs, are always popular. As the systems are based on British Sign Language (BSL), signing is a valuable and marketable skill in the workplace.

Schools that have developed the use of signing find there are benefits for a large number of pupils: those with minor hearing loss caused by colds or glue ear, pupils with receptive language difficulties, and pupils with attention disorders. A visual component added to speech will not impede more able pupils, and will support many others. Signing has the extra benefit of slowing down speech – only a very skilled signer can sign at the rate at which people usually talk. Signing also encourages adults to use more simplified and direct language.

The benefits of signing are, in short:

- it supports receptive and expressive communication;
- it is a valuable skill for all;
- it slows down and simplifies speech;
- it encourages independence and self-advocacy;
- it enables communication between peers;
- it increases participation in school life for pupils with SEND.

Computers

In the past, the hope was that all children with communication or learning difficulties would have access to individual computers that would enable them to communicate and write independently. That is taking rather longer than was originally thought, but the technology is now available to give appropriate technological support to facilitate pupils' communication and to help them access the curriculum.

Basic, inexpensive laptop computers loaded with a speech-to-text software or Clicker 6 will increase independence for pupils with SEND. Adding other software to meet individual needs will support learning across the curriculum. Software such as concept mapping, maths and spelling programs will also help pupils develop basic skills. There are a number of low-cost notebooks and tablets available which are robust and are ideal for use in classrooms and at home. Pupils learn how to use these machines quickly and then are better able to take a full part in lessons. Self-esteem is also improved, especially for pupils in Years 10 and 11. All the information is easily transferred to printers or a memory stick.

Use caution when introducing IT-based learning to pupils with ASD as they may be reluctant to stop working on the machines or will refuse to work on the programs decided by the teacher. This can become a trigger for conflict. A way to avoid this situation is to give the pupil a visual schedule for the lesson and to put the computer work at the end.

The schedule shows the pupil what he or she is expected to do before using the computer. This system also has the added benefit of motivating a pupil to finish any other work first. The bell at the end of the lesson will encourage the pupil to stop and to move on to the next class.

Case study: Jay

Jay is in Year 8. He has a diagnosis of Asperger's syndrome. The school uses a computer-based learning system to support learning for pupils with special needs. Every time Jay uses the program he becomes very excited and aggressive. He always looks forward to the computer sessions, but his teachers are reluctant to let him continue because he has damaged one of the machines.

Patrick, the school SENCO, offered to observe Jay in a computer session before the decision to withdraw him was finalised. Patrick noticed that Jay talked to himself whenever he worked on the computers, becoming increasingly angry. Jay repeatedly came out of the tasks to check his score. As he had only completed part of the task, his score was less than 100 per cent. Patrick quickly realised that Jay was misunderstanding the scoring system and this was the reason for his challenging behaviour. Jay knew he was answering all the questions correctly, but was still scoring less than 100 per cent.

Patrick recommended that Jay work on different programs with a non-accessible scoring system. Jay soon settled into the new programs, and there was no repetition of the challenging behaviour.

Resources

There is a range of equipment that all secondary schools may reasonably be expected to have available to support the learning of pupils with SEND. Much of this equipment is comparatively low cost, and usefully supports many pupils with both temporary and permanent difficulties. Support items include the following:

- writing slopes
- non-slip mats;
- chairs of differing or adjustable heights;
- triangular pen and pencil grips;
- easy-grip scissors;
- tablet or laptop computers;
- stress balls.

Support toolboxes

Some schools provide their teaching assistants with support toolboxes. These small toolboxes might contain a variety of equipment to support pupils in lessons. Much of the equipment in the toolbox is easily available in school, but it is more time-efficient to have it all together and to hand. The toolbox could contain:

camera	voice recorder	stress ball	stickers
stapler	paper fasteners	skipping rope	rubber bands
sticky tape	colouring pad	coins	dominoes
pens and pencils	treasury tags	memory stick	pencil sharpener
small ruler	plastic wallets	highlighter pens	glue stick
paper clips	coloured pens	calculator	counters
scissors	pencil grips	sticky notes	dice or spinners
tissues	eraser	sand timer	playing cards

tools

Figure 5.12 Suggested contents of a support toolbox

Outside agencies

Professionals from other agencies are a fantastic source of information and ideas for support for pupils with SEND. Some professionals such as occupational therapists may work directly with parents. Parents will usually pass on booklets and/or therapy programmes that can be incorporated into staff training or the school timetable. Always try to obtain a copy of a pupil's therapy targets, even if the therapy takes place in a clinic or at home.

As previously highlighted, when planning annual review meetings, invite all the professionals who work with the pupil. The primary purpose of the meeting is to review the pupil's progress against the outcomes in the EHC plan, but the meeting is an ideal forum to share information and advice, and will help professionals from outside education gain an understanding of how the pupil is being included in the school. The nature and level of support can be discussed and amended to give the pupil more help, to develop peer support, or to plan for increased independence as the student moves towards the next phase of education or training.

Summary

When planning support for inclusion, see if you can find additional, more creative ways of supporting pupils who have SEND. Draw on support from other adults and pupils as well as teaching assistants and teachers; this is not only more effective in practice, it is more cost- effective too. The pupil who has SEND benefits from being part of a wider social circle that demands and develops different social skills. Let's consign the 'Velcro' teaching assistant – the practice of teaching assistants sitting next to pupils in all lessons — to history!

Chapter 6 looks at social interaction and behaviour.

Chapter 6

Social interaction and behaviour

Social interaction

A major reason for including pupils with SEND in mainstream schools is the opportunity for social interaction. Among other children of the same age through the secondary school years, pupils with SEND gain good models of appropriate language and behavior, and other pupils in the school learn about disability and become more accepting of diversity in society.

No one can learn to interact merely by being in an occasional PSHE lesson, or in a small speech and language therapy group, although these classes and interventions to some extent will help to develop social skills. Pupils need opportunities to try out what they have learned and to get to know other people of the same age. As pupils move through the school they can become less tolerant of differences and they may be embarrassed to have a person with a disability as a member of their social group. No school should simply accept this situation as inevitable, because it can be remedied. A buddy system or Circle of Friends, as outlined in Chapter 5, will provide a framework on which real relationships can develop. It is highly likely that, depending on the individual pupil's changing level of interaction, such systems will need to be used more than once.

Pupils with SEND sometimes may have hidden talents or interests that the school could use to develop interaction. A pupil may have an excellent singing voice, a love of painting, or be interested in computer games. Often school clubs are a great way to include pupils with SEND in situations that guarantee success and interaction. There may be transport issues when clubs take place after school, but these problems should not be insurmountable.

Case study: Saul

Saul is in Year 10. Saul has a speech and language disorder and associated severe difficulties with literacy. His speech is very difficult to understand, and he spent much of Years 7 and 8 in the special needs unit of the school with little access to the mainstream curriculum. Frequently Saul was teased about his speech. The teasing was quite gentle, but it bothered Saul deeply. He became increasingly withdrawn and was reluctant to go outside the special needs unit.

By the time he reached Year 9, Saul had grown from being a small boy, to a tall well-built young man. Physically he was very fit and had shone in the adapted games he played with the pupils from the special needs unit. The PE teacher invited Saul to join the Year 9 rugby squad for regular training. Almost as soon as he ran on to the field his talent for the game was obvious. He trained twice each week and by the end of the year he was playing for the under-14 team. His speech difficulties mattered very little in the rugby team, and he socialised with the other players in school and in the evening – much to his mother's concern (it was surprising how well he learned to sing the rugby songs on the coach to matches). His speech and his general abilities improved overall.

Grouping for inclusion

To be able to learn and play alongside their chronological peers is a vital part of inclusion for pupils with SEND. There are no lessons on how to be a teenager – children work this out for themselves by being together, talking, listening to music, watching older pupils being cool, and by distancing themselves from the younger ones. Without this everyday contact a pupil with SEND becomes even more different – in how they dress, their interests, even in the words they use. Adults can be very caring and well-meaning, but they no longer have the 'social code' of young people.

Pupils with SEND need to have the experiences, resources, materials and activities that would be expected for any other pupil of the same age. In class, a pupil with significant learning difficulties may still be working on objectives from Key Stage 1 or 2, but that does not mean they have to use primary workbooks. The content of the work and the objectives may be from Key Stage 1, but the context, materials and the expectations of how the student should work, should be radically different.

Which year group?

The right group for a pupil with SEND is one where they are with children they already know – from their previous school or from the local neighbourhood. The criteria are the same that all schools use to group pupils transferring from primary. These criteria are far more important than class size or the amount of support available; SEND is not in itself a reason to segregate. Grouping pupils with others who they already know will help them settle more quickly and effectively into a new environment and, so placed, their classmates will be a natural source of continuity and support.

Where children move to a new school with which they have no links, the school will need to work extra hard to help to develop social relationships. A buddy system or Circle of Friends approach will give a basis for relationships and help pupils to develop the skills and strategies necessary to become part of their peer group. Schools sometimes decide to 'wait and see' for a few weeks to see how the pupil gets on with the others, but this is rarely successful. Much more effective is a proactive approach from the beginning, which makes the class a more cohesive group and benefits everyone in it.

Personal, social and health education

Although personal, social and health education (PSHE) is a non-statutory subject and no standardised programmes of study are provided for schools, it remains an important and necessary part of all pupils' education. All schools have a duty to provide a curriculum that is broadly based, balanced and that meets the needs of all pupils and:

- promotes the spiritual, moral, cultural, mental and physical development of pupils at the school and of society, and
- prepares pupils for the opportunities, responsibilities and experiences of later life.

PSHE schemes of work provide ideal opportunities in which to focus on such priorities as eliminating bullying, and addressing all forms of prejudice, including the use of prejudice-based language, and developing a greater acceptance of diversity, both in school and in society as a whole. These schemes of work will set the framework for the development of more inclusive attitudes and practices, and underpin the development of resilience for more vulnerable students. Many of these aspects can be addressed not only through the PSHE programme, but also in the way the school supports inclusive attitudes and behaviour among students, and between pupils and staff. Students will take their lead from the adults around them, and how members of staff show respect and tolerance for pupils with SEND is of great importance. Being part of a buddy system or a Circle of Friends will do much more to develop pupils' understanding of diversity, social justice and fairness than any number of lessons.

Behaviour

Very rarely does a pupil with SEND have behaviour difficulties attributable directly to his or her learning disability. When pupils are offered age-appropriate activities at which they can succeed, behaviour difficulties will be kept to a minimum. As with all pupils, those with SEND will behave the better in situations where they feel confident and valued. When the work they are expected to complete is far too complex – or far too easy – behaviour will deteriorate. Challenging behaviour is almost always the pupils' response to the demands made on them and on their environment. It is not necessarily an inherent problem within the pupil, or their SEND, but rather an indicator of how a pupil feels about school. When behaviour deteriorates suddenly there is always a reason. Impulsive or irrational behaviour occurs when pupils do not know what to do in a situation, and is usually a sign of severe anxiety. Sending the pupil to stand outside the room, shouting, or exhortations to 'be good' will not be effective ways of dealing with the situation. It is important to look for the reason behind the behaviour and, if possible, address the cause of the problem. Observe the pupil in different lessons, and at various times of the day. It is possible that, as with Jason in the example below, he is 'playing to the gallery' or copying others. Find out what is triggering the behaviour and ask parents if they have noticed any changes at home.

When there is more than one adult in a lesson, the teacher needs to be responsible (and to be seen by pupils to be so) for the learning and behaviour of all the pupils in the class, even those pupils supported one-to-one by a teaching assistant. Pupils are very quick to work out who has the authority in any situation, and can behave very differently for a teacher than they do for a teaching assistant.

Case study: Jason

Jason is in Year 9. He finds it very difficult to manage his anxiety in noisy situations and has frequent panic attacks. During the fourth week of the school year Jason began to behave strangely in science. Either he bit his nails constantly and growled when anyone came near him, or he hopped around the room like a rabbit. The science teacher reported these behaviours to the SENCO and Jason awaited assessment by the educational psychologist.

When the SENCO investigated Jason's behaviour, she found that he was in a bottom set for science. The majority of pupils in the class were boys who had behavioural difficulties. These boys laughed at Jason when he misbehaved, but he appeared to like the attention. The science teacher was in his second year of teaching. His lessons were not differentiated because the pupils were in sets for science. The teacher never spoke directly to Jason.

The SENCO arranged for Jason to transfer to a higher science set with a more experienced teacher. This teacher worked with the SENCO to prepare differentiated activities. Jason worked with a partner or in small groups for each lesson and was given praise by the teacher when he was on task. His behaviour and achievement improved immediately.

The best way of learning why pupils use inappropriate behaviour is to observe them and identify 'flashpoints' – times in the school day when a pupil's behaviour becomes less appropriate. An ABC (Antecedents, Behaviours and Consequences) assessment of situations can be undertaken, preferably by a colleague who does not currently teach the pupil, and so relatively dispassionate. This assessment should give a clearer understanding of the behaviours and provide clues as to how to move forward.

Antecedents

Identify what might have led to the inappropriate behaviour. For example:

- Does the behaviour happen before or during some lessons more than others?
- Are particular pupils regularly involved?
- Could there be any sensory reasons for the behaviour (such as the noise of computers or a flickering fluorescent light)?

Behaviour

Describe the exact nature of the inappropriate behaviour.

- Be precise when describing behaviour as the differences may reflect differing reasons. For example, running out of class may be because the pupil is anxious or afraid, whereas running around the room may be to gain an adult's attention.

Consequences

Describe what happened as a consequence of the behaviour.

- How did the pupil react?
- How did other pupils react?
- How did the adults in the room react?
- Was the pupil punished? If so, how?
- Did the pupil receive the pay-off he or she wanted?
- Were there any long-term consequences, such as parents being informed?

An ABC observation form (Figure 6.1) follows.

For many pupils, attention from adults is the need underlying the inappropriate behaviour. When children do not get the positive attention they need they will make sure they get *some* attention – negative or positive – in the only way they know will work for certain, by using inappropriate behaviour. To ignore inappropriate behaviour really goes against the grain for teachers and teaching assistants. They feel that if they ignore the behaviour the pupil is 'getting away with it' and that it is unfair to other pupils. But ignoring some behaviours does work – eventually. For this approach to be truly effective the adults involved must remove all attention and communication from the pupil – don't even glance at him or her. Other pupils usually are sufficiently aware (without feeling that they have to try it too) to understand that teachers are trying to change the inappropriate behaviour.

When a pupil's behaviour becomes either too disruptive or too dangerous you will have to do something. The most effective course of action is to divert the pupil's attention. Ask him or her to do something for you, either in the classroom or in another part of the school. Changing the dynamics of a situation in this way will give the pupil a way out of a difficult situation and usually restores order. Do not show that you are irritated or bothered by the behaviour. Stay emotionally neutral, with a calm voice and relaxed demeanour, which is very hard for a teacher to do when faced with challenging behaviour, but this is very important and very effective. Anger management techniques may be appropriate for some pupils, and information and advice can be sought from a behaviour support team or educational psychologist.

To remind pupils of how they should behave, behaviour prompt pictures or symbols can be effective. Symbols such as 'be quiet', 'wait' or 'sit down' can be held towards the pupil by the teacher or teaching assistant (see Figure 6.2). This method is particularly useful where a teaching assistant is observing and supporting the whole class. The prompts can be used for any pupil who needs a reminder, and the cards do not necessarily require any additional comment or action. If symbols are to be used the pupils will need to learn their meanings, but they will then be useful for all pupils, including those with literacy difficulties.

Giving a pupil a message to take to another member of staff often works well: the school receptionist or headteacher's secretary are the ideal recipients for the note, mainly because they are usually located close to the headteacher's office. Arrange beforehand that if the pupil arrives at the office with a piece of paper, he or she should be thanked and asked to wait for a few minutes. The pupil then is asked to return the note to the teacher. By the time the pupil returns the situation in the class will have been defused and the other pupils will have settled down to work. Pupils with SEND are rarely given even small responsibilities, and just taking a note to the office will build up self-esteem.

ABC Record	Name:	Class/Year group:	Date:
Pupil's strengths and interests:			
Antecedents: what happens before the behaviours?	Behaviours: describe the behaviours		Consequences: what happens after the behaviours?
What is the pupil trying to communicate?	What prevention strategies are in place?		What alternative behaviours are being taught?

Figure 6.1 Template for ABC observation form

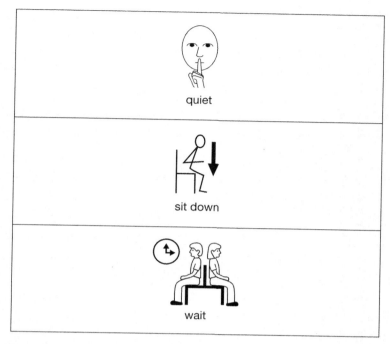

quiet

sit down

wait

Figure 6.2 Behaviour prompt cards

The pupil also has a break in concentration and gets a little physical exercise. Most pupils return to class having forgotten the previous difficulties. A teaching assistant might escort the pupil to the office or other classroom, but it is better if he or she goes alone. If there are any safety concerns the teaching assistant could shadow the pupil from a distance. Dealing with disruptive behaviour in this way causes minimal disruption for the teacher, the class or the individual pupil. It also helps teachers to feel they are not alone in tackling disruptive behaviour and encourages co-operation between colleagues.

Wherever possible, ignore low-level aggravation. Instead, accentuate and praise anything that is positive. This does take time to work, but in the end will have the desired effect. When giving praise minimise the language used, so that the pupil knows exactly what is good behaviour. Phrases such as 'good listening', 'good watching' or 'neat writing' are perfect when said with a smile. Pupils eventually learn which behaviours are acceptable and which are not. This 'shower of affirmation' approach is very powerful and will transform a pupil's behaviour.

It is always worth trying to accentuate the positive, because the alternative is the 'he or she mustn't get away with it' approach, with a stream of corrections and reprimands. Reprimands quickly lose effect when a pupil constantly is being told off and getting the attention they crave – albeit negative attention. That situation then escalates with the pupil becoming an increasing nuisance in classes and needing increasingly severe sanctions. This is in no one's interest and only serves to make teachers and teaching assistants stressed, and the pupil with SEND unhappy and confused.

Some schools provide training for staff in positive physical intervention/restraint. Restraint is necessary only with very few pupils in equally few situations, usually following badly handled confrontations with pupils, and should only ever be a short-term measure discussed and agreed with parents beforehand. Where adults do not feel able to 'back down' so that a pupil does not 'get the upper hand', there can be no winners. People with SEND are very rarely deliberately vindictive or aggressive.

Inevitably there will be occasions when behaviour goes beyond low-level aggravation and some form of verbal chastisement is needed. The correction should take place immediately, but in any case as soon as possible after the incident has occurred. If you wait until the end of the lesson, or even the end of the day, the pupil may well have forgotten what happened and will not understand why they are being chastised. Much more effective will be simple language and short phrases immediately expressed. When angry, our vocal tone rises, we speak more quickly, and we use more complex words and sentence structures, including irony and sarcasm. Pupils who have comprehension difficulties, which category includes many children with SEND, will likely not understand what is being said. These pupils then actively switch off, with the speech becoming simply a wash of sound.

Use a form of words that condemns the inappropriate behaviour rather than the child, such as 'Don't tear pages from your book. If you need spare paper, get it from my desk.' Being told that they are 'naughty' or 'bad' does not help pupils to change behaviours and can seriously damage self-esteem, confidence and motivation. Tell the pupil what they did that was wrong, and then tell them what they should have done; when they know how to behave there will be a greater likelihood of future compliance.

Before beginning to tell them off, wherever possible take the pupil to a private place. Dressing-down a pupil in public should be a thing of the past, especially for someone with SEND who may react in a less mature way. Embarrassment will reduce the pupil's motivation to learn and tend to make him or her less willing to interact with peers.

Make your requirements to the pupil explicit. Let the pupil know exactly how you expect them to behave – what they *should* do in the situation. All teachers have slightly different expectations of pupil behaviour. For example, pupils can talk in some subjects but not in others, and what does 'talking quietly' mean? Teachers may need to repeat their own expectations many times. Social norms that most people take for granted, such as holding doors open for others, may not be known or understood by pupils with SEND. These norms need to be taught explicitly.

Moving around school between lessons is a complex and challenging situation, both socially and intellectually. Holding the door open may be the last thing on the pupil's mind and may simply be forgotten. Show the pupil how to hold the door open and explain when it should be closed. Something this simple frequently causes pupils with SEND to be in trouble with teachers or prefects, but they usually have no idea what they have done to cause them to be told off or punished.

Rules

Pupils with SEND generally like to obey school rules, but in order to follow rules pupils have to know and understand them. When rules are clear and unambiguous, they give a sense of structure and order. School rules usually are written down in a prospectus or in homework planners and for most pupils that is sufficient. Pupils with SEND, however, may need opportunities to learn the school rules and time to discuss them with an adult. Only when this has been done should pupils with SEND be expected to know and obey school rules.

Some pupils need to have additional, individual rules that will help them manage their own behaviour in situations they find difficult. A pupil with SEND may not know such things as:

- hands must be raised before speaking to the teacher;
- walk rather than run in the corridors;
- money is needed to buy a snack;
- ask before borrowing someone else's rubber or ruler.

Written down in the pupil's planner can be a few specific personal rules. These rules can be shared with a teaching assistant or pupil mentor in registration and form periods. The pupil's parents and all subject teachers should have a copy. Frequently these individual rules can deflect potential misdemeanours, and they take little time and effort to put in place. When the pupil knows and understands what is expected, he or she can then be subject to the usual school sanctions.

When unacceptable behaviour is repeated, offer practical alternatives. For example, when a pupil always throws her pen down on to the desk, provide a desk tidy where the pen can be placed. Such a simple action can defuse a potentially explosive situation. Dealing with the quantity of 'stuff' they have with them can be overwhelming for some pupils. Those with an Autistic Spectrum Disorder may spend much of a lesson setting out all their pens, felt-tips, rubbers, rulers, protractor, set square, etc. – and this in geography! It is not that the pupil wants to do this, but they do not know what equipment is important for each different lesson, so everything comes out and has to be placed in the right order. A simple list of words, symbols or small photographs of what is needed for each subject can very quickly solve the problem.

Where a pupil uses several unacceptable behaviours in school, attempt to change only one behaviour at a time. Tell the pupil what needs to change and teach an acceptable alternative. Make regular notes on the changes in the pupil's behaviour. This may seem like excessive record keeping, but when teachers and teaching assistants can see a pupil making improvements in behaviour, they begin to feel better about both themselves and the pupil. It can be easy to miss genuine improvements in a pupil's behaviour without noting down the changes. Any improvements should be celebrated with the pupil, and with their parents, and among staff. Changing the staff's perceptions of a pupil is often as important as changing the pupil's behaviour. 'Once a nuisance always a nuisance' can be the attitude, even when the pupil's behaviour has improved dramatically.

Whole-staff understanding

Where there are adults in the school who do not understand the reasons for a pupil's behaviour, a negative or angry response from just one adult can cause a pupil great distress and undo many months of progress. Pupils with SEND often will have no behaviour difficulties in class, but may experience conflicts with other pupils at lunchtimes or breaks. It requires a high level of understanding and skill to manage such situations. Lunchtime supervisors, administrators or cleaning staff rarely have specific training in behaviour management and usually have to rely on their own experiences of school or of raising children. Inappropriate management can cause minor arguments to become major incidents. The following case study is an example.

Case study: Chrissie

Chrissie is in Year 8. There was a disturbance on Chrissie's lunch table. The lunchtime supervisor, Mrs Jones, went over to investigate the problem. She saw Chrissie rocking in her seat and repeatedly trying to take a chocolate bar from the boy sitting next to her. Mrs Jones told Chrissie to stop rocking and to leave the boy alone. Chrissie stood up and began to cry and shout. Mrs Jones took hold of her arm and encouraged her to sit down again, and to continue eating. At this Chrissie lashed out and again grabbed at the chocolate bar the boy was now eating. In lashing out she struck Mrs Jones on the face. Mrs Jones was clearly shocked and upset, and shouted at Chrissie who then tried to run out of the hall. A teacher and a teaching assistant restrained Chrissie before she could leave the hall. She fell to the floor and refused to get up. The two adults then spent the next hour sitting on the dining-hall floor trying unsuccessfully to calm Chrissie down. Eventually her mother was called and she went home.

Chrissie arrived back in school the next day and behaved as if nothing had happened.

The original commotion at the table was because the boy next to Chrissie had 'swapped' his biscuit for her chocolate bar. She had used her limited language skills to ask for it back. The boy had refused and the whole table was laughing at Chrissie's response of rocking and grabbing at the chocolate bar. By the time she was reprimanded by Mrs Jones, Chrissie had become really upset. An aspect of Chrissie's SEND is that she is tactile defensive – she does not like being touched. When Mrs Jones took her arm she reacted instinctively because of her emotional state and lashed out. She had not meant to harm Mrs Jones, but when shouted at, her instinct had been to get away from the situation as quickly as possible. When stopped and held by two adults the sensory overload was too great for Chrissie and she then dropped to the floor, curling into the foetal position. This was not Chrissie behaving badly – it was a survival technique.

In this situation Chrissie did not know what she had done wrong, nor did she understand why Mrs Jones was angry. The comment in the incident book notes that Chrissie's behaviour was violent and aggressive and that she needed to be restrained. The boy who enjoyed her chocolate bar also enjoyed the entertainment.

If training had been given before Chrissie arrived at the school, this situation would likely have been more sensitively handled. Mrs Jones would have known that Chrissie did not like to be touched, and recognised her rocking as a sign of anxiety.

Harness the skills of lunchtime supervisors, administration staff and even the caretaker, and this will pay dividends by minimising escalating behaviours in less structured school settings.

Safe havens

Many schools now create safe havens for vulnerable pupils. This may be a room or an area in the school where pupils can choose to go at break and lunchtimes to stay safe, keep out of trouble, calm down, or just catch up on work. It is vital that the safe haven is staffed by experienced teachers and teaching assistants. Safe havens are often a valuable way to support pupils with SEND, especially those with emotional, social and mental health difficulties. Pupils can prepare for their next lessons, or get support with homework. The resources needed for a safe haven are minimal – a few board-games, paper and pens, and books are all that is necessary. The staff member is the most important resource and being on duty in the safe haven is usually a pleasant experience.

Equal and realistic expectations

Do make sure that you have realistic expectations of how a pupil with SEND should and could behave. Each person has his or her own personality traits and quirks which may annoy others. Some pupils with SEND have physical tics that they cannot control. Some pupils hum quietly – or not so quietly – when they are concentrating. Others may make noises intermittently or have stereotypical behaviours, such as turning around before they sit down. These individual traits will need to be taken into account before a pupil's behaviour can be described as disruptive.

Because they have special educational needs, pupils with SEND are watched much more closely than other pupils. Teachers and teaching assistants make sure they stay on task throughout lessons. Monitoring the time that all pupils stay on task will give a more accurate picture of how hard the pupil with SEND is working in comparison with others. Most pupils *without* SEND 'attend' only intermittently, sometimes listening or working, at other times looking out of the window or chatting to a friend. Be sure not to expect higher standards of behaviour from pupils with SEND than those you expect from other students. A valuable source of information on really how well a pupil is performing in lessons are observations by colleagues.

Can't or won't

Teachers are great communicators, very skilled in speaking to and with pupils and in assessing their moods and intentions. Knowing whether a pupil is unable to do work, or is simply refusing to try, is always difficult to determine. A teacher gauges the pupil's response from what they say, how they say it, from eye contact, from facial expression and from body language. All this information, combined with previous knowledge of a pupil's work, determines the teacher's response. Is the pupil to be given extra help or a detention?

With pupils with SEND it is less straightforward. Pupils with SEND may appear to be refusing to attempt the work, or to be taking an inordinately long time over it. It may be impossible for a pupil to say why the work has not been done. Often pupils with SEND smile at the teacher when asked why they haven't finished their work. This can be misconstrued as defiance or plain rudeness. The pupil probably is truly perplexed. The teacher is someone the pupil likes, so when the teacher speaks, the pupil smiles. At this point the pupil is probably not listening to the words spoken by the teacher, but looking at and trying to decipher his or her facial expression. When the teacher becomes angry or gives a detention the pupil often has no idea of the reason. For many pupils with SEND, eye contact, facial expression and body language are not often sufficiently sophisticated to transmit such complex feelings precisely. In this situation misunderstandings are common and lead to distress on all sides.

'Manipulative' pupils?

Teachers report frequently that pupils with SEND are 'manipulative'. When investigated this adjective is found to mean that the pupil wants to get their own way. If this is the case, then the pupil with SEND is no different from any other child or young person. All children want their own way. Children learn as they grow that they have to wait or conform to adult requests. They still want their own way, but most also want to please adults. Pupils with SEND will take longer to learn this particular social skill. They may not necessarily want to please a particular adult and are likely to have access only to more immature strategies.

Case study: Sian

Sian is in Year 9. She loves all lessons, except Mrs Phillips's design and technology classes. She finds the noises of the machines very frightening, but has so far managed to remain relatively calm, and has stayed in the lessons. For the past three weeks, though, Sian has used a number of tactics first not to go to the lesson, and second as often as possible to get out of the workshop. The first week Sian said she had a headache and was allowed to stay in the library. On the second week she asked six times to go to the toilet. On the third occasion Sian kept returning to her form room, saying she had forgotten various items of equipment, her pen, her design folder, etc.

The teaching assistant in the science department realised that something was wrong and spoke to Sian at dinnertime. When the teaching assistant mentioned the workshop Sian immediately began to cry. Mrs Phillips arranged for a small group including Sian to work in another room on the weeks when the machines were in use. Sian's behaviour gradually improved and she will now tolerate some noise in the workshops.

Tiredness

In order to understand and respond to lessons in school, pupils with SEND have to work very hard. The effort they expend will be greater than almost any other pupil in the class. Once most pupils learn a routine they hardly need to think about it, whereas pupils with SEND need to think about almost everything, every time. They can take little for granted. This is another reason why visual cues and lists are so useful. They need to remember and actively think about such things as how to get to the next lesson, the equipment they will need for each activity and catching the school bus home. This constant, active thinking in addition to the school work and the effort of social interaction causes pupils with SEND to become very tired by the end of the school day.

Tiredness will also have an impact on the amount and quality of homework that pupils with SEND will be able to complete. If parents report that their child is becoming anxious about homework, consider setting less, or give the pupil a time extension. Teachers will get the best from pupils with SEND during the school day if those pupils have had a chance to rest during the previous evening. Homework clubs held immediately after school can be a useful support, and staff will be better able to gauge whether a pupil really is too tired to do the homework, or is just reluctant to work. When pupils are genuinely too tired to complete homework, provide them with something else to do at home, whether collecting objects, reading a passage or watching a film of a set work. It is important that other pupils do not see that a fellow pupil is 'getting away with' homework, and the pupil with SEND needs to keep up a pattern of working at home.

The impact of illness on behaviour

As with all pupils, the behaviour of pupils with SEND will change when they have an illness. Unfortunately, it is not possible to anticipate how the behaviour will change. Some pupils become very withdrawn and quiet, others have the opposite reaction. Try always to investigate so as to find out if illness could be the cause of negative changes in a pupil's behaviour. Often a telephone call to parents will answer concerns before a difficult situation develops in school.

Case study: Jackson

Jackson is in Year 7 and has severe and complex SEND. He usually behaves well in school, but he is sometimes wilful and can refuse to do as he is asked.

At the start of the spring term, Jackson's behaviour deteriorated rapidly. He became increasingly resistant to requests to work, and he was verbally and physically abusive to the teachers, teaching assistants, and other pupils. Jackson's behaviour was also very challenging at home, especially as he no longer slept through the night. He appeared unhappy and anxious. His parents put his behaviour down to the hormonal changes of puberty. In the week before half-term Jackson kicked and injured a teacher's leg. In line with school policy Jackson was given a temporary exclusion, and several teachers and parents lobbied the governors to have him removed from the school permanently.

Jackson's parents were very concerned and so took him to see the family doctor. The doctor discovered that Jackson had a very serious ear infection that would have caused him continual discomfort. He was given antibiotics and after a few days his behaviour returned to normal.

Jackson did not have the language skills to express the pain he was experiencing. His only way of showing the distress was through his behaviour.

This case study is not to condone Jackson's behaviour, but to explain why the incidents occurred.

Medication

For conditions such as epilepsy, some pupils with SEND will need to take medicines. It may take several months for doctors to perfect the choice and dosage of medication for a particular individual, and the pupil's behaviour is likely to be erratic during this time. Communication with parents is obviously of vital importance in this situation, and school staff will need to be understanding and more tolerant of unusual behaviour.

Potential difficulties in non-directed time

Most pupils with SEND quickly learn how to behave in lessons. They become familiar and comfortable in the structured settings and behave accordingly. Problems frequently arise in less structured times in school, such as the transitions between lessons, breaks and lunchtimes. The problems often arise because of misunderstandings between students or because the pupil does not know what they are expected to do and how they should behave. During breaks, the buddy system or Circle of Friends (see Chapter 5) will support pupils with SEND. Members of the Circle of Friends inviting the pupil to join games in the playground, or talking to him or her, will often make the world of difference to a pupil's behaviour and confidence.

Do not assign a teaching assistant to accompany a pupil with SEND in breaks and lunchtimes. An adult trailing round serves only to make the pupil appear to be more different from other pupils, and makes interaction much less likely. However, the extra teaching assistant could join other staff on the rota for the safe haven. This use of support hours would be preferable and far more effective than having the teaching assistant shepherd the pupil in the playground. Some headteachers refer to one-to-one teaching assistants as 'minders' and sometimes it is easy to see why.

Because it is that very lack of structure that causes some pupils to behave inappropriately, problems in unstructured times are the most difficult to resolve. Pupils with SEND need three elements of structure to be in place. These elements are:

- social
- physical
- time.

Social

It may be that the pupil with SEND cannot cope with the social demands of breaks. Lining up to buy a drink, trying to join a game or returning a library book involves meeting and interacting with many people, adults and pupils. The pupil with SEND has to remember how to address and respond to each different person. A number of such fleeting interactions in a short period of time can overload the pupil with SEND, cause anxiety or overexcitement, and lead to inappropriate behaviour. Limiting the social demands will help pupils, especially when they are new to the school. For example, the drink or snack could be paid for by parents in advance, and the pupil could collect it from the tuck shop without queuing. Once again, the buddy system or Circle of Friends offers support and provides a consistent friendly face.

Problems arise when pupils with SEND copy the behaviours of other pupils in less appropriate ways. This is the case especially when they copy the physical play of younger children.

Physical

Secondary schools are large and complex communities: different buildings with different purposes, but frequently without signs. Signs with words and symbols will help both pupils and visitors find their way around independently. Outside areas often are even more confusing – large open areas without demarcations. They often adjoin the school field without a fence or other boundary. This space is wonderful for most pupils because they have the freedom to run around and play football etc., but that very space can cause huge anxieties for some pupils with SEND. They may want to run but will not know when to stop, and then could go outside the school boundary (and break another school rule in the process).

Case study: Mandev

Mandev is in Year 8. He spends most breaks walking around the edge of the play area or sitting on the steps. In recent days he has been in trouble for 'assaulting' other pupils and a teaching assistant. These unprovoked attacks (as they were described in the school incident book) took the form of Mandev jumping on to the back of his 'victim' and hanging on until forcibly removed.

Fortunately, Mandev's classmate had seen several of the incidents and he suggested that his form teacher go outside to see for himself. The boy had observed that Mandev's behaviour happened after he had been watching a group of boys play. The game consisted of a boy jumping on to a friend's back and being swung around to cause him to fall off. The rest of the group cheered them on.

Mandev had watched the game and had seen how the boys enjoyed themselves. He copied their game because he wanted to have fun. He did not understand that he should have asked if the other pupils – mostly girls – wanted to play the game, and he certainly could not understand why everyone was so angry with him.

Some pupils with SEND can become distressed in very cold or very hot weather, and so may behave inappropriately. Physically they may not be able to regulate their body temperature, or they may be unable to match their clothing to the weather conditions.

Most of these problems can be avoided by giving the pupil with SEND something to do during breaktimes: going to choir, helping in the office, joining a board game or art club, or reading in the library. Activities such as these will avoid outside behaviour difficulties and will support the pupil's developing social skills.

Time

Pupils with SEND may not have a complete understanding of time. Breaks on a freezing day are bearable, because we know that we can go back into the warmth in fifteen minutes. Most pupils know how long fifteen minutes lasts and they use that sense of time to anticipate when the bell will ring. Pupils with SEND may not have that ability and for them that cold break might go on forever. They cannot anticipate the end of unpalatable situations, and so behave in the way most likely to make the situation stop. By behaving inappropriately they get to go inside, where social, physical and temporal boundaries are much clearer.

Structuring lunchtimes and breaks will give pupils support they need, and a picture or symbol timetable is often all that is needed. The timetable gives a temporal framework to the unstructured time and also tells the pupil what to do. The timetable can be in words and/or symbols and should be set out to cover either each day or a week, depending on the level of understanding of the pupil.

The following timetable is for Siobhan in Year 10. She is on first sitting for dinner on Monday, Tuesday and Wednesday, but on second sitting on Thursday and Friday. This causes her huge problems, as frequently she goes into the wrong sitting and becomes distressed when told that she has to wait. This timetable is reviewed every two weeks. The timetable was drawn up by Siobhan and a teaching assistant. Siobhan chose the activities and when she wanted to do them.

Day	Break	Dinner	
Monday	Computer	Canteen	Library
Tuesday	Board games	Canteen	Choir
Wednesday	Library	Canteen	Art club
Thursday	Computer	Office	Canteen
Friday	Band	Library	Canteen

Clock faces can be added to the timetable to let pupils know when to go to clubs or back to class. More information and/or symbols might be added depending on the understanding of the individual pupil.

The vocabulary of feelings

In order to effect changes in our behaviour we need to be able to think about, and understand, why we behave in certain ways. Underpinning that understanding is a wide vocabulary of words relating to emotions. We have access to a wonderfully rich and complex language through which we express and consider our feelings in precise detail. Adolescent girls in particular spend much of their free time discussing how they feel and how other people make them feel. They pick up on unspoken cues from other people and give friends emotional support by empathising with their problems.

The limited language that is available to pupils with SEND denies them the full ability to reflect and think through the reasons for their own behaviours, and these pupils do not have an understanding of how their behaviour makes other people feel.

Schools should build opportunities into the curriculum so that pupils with SEND may develop a wider vocabulary of feelings. This vocabulary does not have to be taught separately from other subjects, but a pupil's form tutor or key worker could check that all opportunities available are maximised. For example, in Year 9 history, lessons on the French Revolutionary wars can include discussions on how the peasants felt when they were cold and hungry, how the aristocracy felt when they were in hiding, etc., and the words used could then be recorded in a book or on disk and reviewed in the regular mentor session.

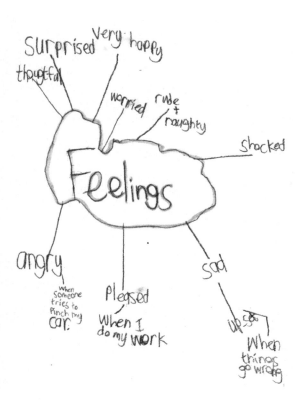

Figure 6.3 Feelings web

Narratives

Narratives are stories written by an adult who knows a pupil well. The narrative helps the pupil to understand situations they find difficult. They let the pupil know what to expect and explain how to behave. The narratives should be short, and can include photographs, drawings and symbols. The story needs to give the pupil information about where and when the situation occurs, who is involved, what usually happens and why. Sometimes reading just two or three sentences regularly with the pupil can prompt changes in understanding and behaviour.

Box 6.1 Example of a narrative

At breaktimes most students go outside. When it has been raining, we all have to stay on the concrete area. This is because the grass gets muddy and makes our shoes and clothes dirty. My mum feels annoyed when my clothes get muddy. I will stay on the concrete area at breaktimes. Mrs Williams or Mrs Smith will tell me when I can go on the grass.

Summary

The major reason for the breakdown in placements for pupils with SEND in mainstream secondary schools is inappropriate or challenging behaviour. Yet the problems lie rarely within the pupil, but are caused mostly by inflexible or inappropriate school systems. Schools must adapt to meet more diverse needs – diverse in terms of learning styles and behaviour – in order to cater for greater diversity among pupils. Taking time to observe and talk to the individual pupil to find the underlying causes of the behaviour will often throw up relatively simple and practical solutions.

The voice of the pupil with SEND is explored in Chapter 7.

Chapter 7

The voice of the pupil with SEND

'The child has a right to express an opinion and to have that opinion taken into account, in any matter or procedure affecting the child.'

(Article 12 of the United Nations Convention on the Rights of the Child, 1990)

Parents, teachers, doctors, psychologists, therapists – we always *speak for* the child with SEND, but we rarely listen to what he or she has to say. The United Nations Convention on the Rights of the Child (1990) makes clear that we must begin to listen much more directly to the voice of the child, and the child's views must be given due weight when decisions are being made about his or her future.

Well-meaning adults believe they know what is best for children with SEND. For too long the relationship between schools and children and young people with SEND has been based on sympathy. To begin to look at the world through the eyes of the pupil with SEND schools must move away from the paternalistic, sympathetic approach. It may be problematic for schools to adapt to meet the needs of a pupil with SEND, but those problems are as nothing compared to the problems faced every day by that pupil – problems of inaccessible lessons, chaotic corridors, dangerous playgrounds, insensitive people. The time has come for schools and associated professions to adopt a more empathetic stance, with the pupil with SEND at the centre of thinking and planning.

Appreciating that each child is an individual, with distinctive gifts, talents, strengths, abilities, and needs, will help schools become more responsive to the learning needs of all pupils. Part of the appreciation should be an acceptance that pupils with SEND have opinions about school, that they really do have something to say and that it is worth taking the time to listen. Many schools are becoming more democratic and collaborative, with school councils giving pupils a genuine voice in the decision-making processes that affect them. By developing and opening up this process to pupils who experience barriers to participation, schools will gain an added understanding of pupils' perspectives, and the additional participation will increase pupil motivation and limit potential emotional, social and mental health difficulties.

Developing the pupil's voice

Pupils with SEND have to learn how to be active participants in decision making about their own lives and need support from the adults who work with them. A process of preparation can start before the pupil with SEND transfers to the school. Schools give out a lot of information to parents and pupils, and they receive a wealth of information about a pupil's learning. Few schools ask pupils (especially those with SEND) what they want from their time in the secondary school.

Secondary schools could ask new pupils:

- which clubs they would like to have available;
- the sports they enjoy playing;
- the food they like to eat for lunch;
- the books they are reading;
- the software they find useful.

These questions could be in the form of a questionnaire (see Figure 7.1), made accessible through symbols or pictures, in addition to text, to all. Such consultation at this basic level instils in all pupils an expectation of participation and a belief that their opinions are valued. There needs to be determination from parents, teachers and other professionals to provide opportunities for pupils throughout their years in school to make choices and set targets for themselves.

Involve pupils with SEND in group activities and discussions such as brainstorming, examining the pros and cons of a situation and prioritising. This will support the development of pupils' abilities to make informed judgements based on thinking skills. To help pupils develop understanding and empathy for another person's perspective discuss issues raised in books with small groups of their peers.

Circle time

Circle time is valuable for pupils with SEND in many ways. An emphasis on taking turns, affirmation, and particularly listening, supports the development of social and communication skills. If pupils have regular practice in speaking to a group and having what they say respected, they will be the more able to express their opinions and views in other situations, such as annual review meetings.

Reflection and self-assessment

Pupils with SEND need to learn regularly to assess and reflect upon their own performance in school. Where pupils have clear and appropriate objectives for units of work they can judge for themselves whether they have achieved the objectives, and say what they did and did not enjoy about the topic, and say what they found difficult. A completed reflection or self-assessment record for each unit of work could be added to a pupil's progress file or other record of achievement. This information is useful for future planning and differentiation. Over time, supported self-assessment will build up a pupil's confidence, and he or she will learn the skills required to offer opinions on his or her own work, and also on the curricular and social aspects of school. This reflection and self-assessment process will prepare pupils for setting their own academic and social targets.

A pro forma (Figure 7.2) that can be used to support self-assessment follows.

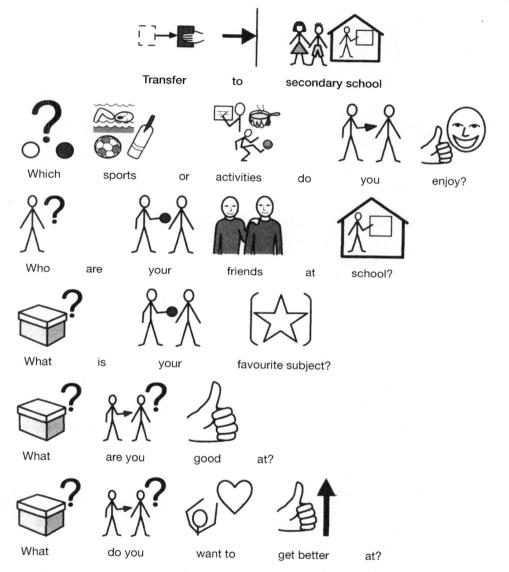

Figure 7.1 Secondary transfer questionnaire

Name _____   Date_____   Subject _____

What I have learned	
What I can now do	
What I enjoyed	
What I found hard	
What I want to do better in the future	
Who helped me	

Figure 7.2 Self-assessment pro-forma

© 2016 *Meeting Special Educational Needs in Secondary Classrooms*, Sue Briggs, Routledge

Advocacy

Many pupils with SEND will be keen to attend meetings in person once they have been prepared in advance (so knowing what to expect). Pupils who are more vulnerable may find the situation too intimidating or distressing, and the use of an advocate is a way of ensuring the young person's voice is heard. An advocate must be someone with no professional or emotional link to the pupil. This person will need to spend time with the pupil, getting to know his or her personality, preferences and opinions about school, and the decisions that have to be made. In the meeting the advocate speaks for the pupil, ensuring the child's voice carries sufficient weight. The pupil's parents must be consulted and they must agree to advocacy before any action is taken.

The advocate could be another pupil in the school. Older pupils often are excellent advocates for pupils with SEND, but before taking on the role they themselves will need preparation and training. The pupil advocate needs to have a very strong personality to put forward the views of a pupil with SEND if his or her views differ from those of the professionals at a meeting. A shared advocacy between a pupil and an adult can also work well, with the pupil giving the 'cultural' balance of young people that the adult will have lost.

Parents as advocates

Parents are natural advocates for their own children, but the wishes of the parents may not necessarily be in accord with the wishes of the child, particularly during adolescence. For parents, their child's need for care, protection and support can override other concerns. Adolescents themselves may have a quite different agenda, possibly involving greater freedom and risk-taking. These differences must be addressed before important decisions are made about a pupil's future. Article 12 of the UN Convention on the Rights of the Child gives the right to express an opinion to the child, rather than to the parent. Whereas parents must always be part of any decision the child has an at least equal right to be heard. For young people over the age of 16, this right is also enshrined in the Children and Family Act 2014 as outlined in the SEND Code of Practice:

> After compulsory school age (the end of the academic year in which they turn 16) the right to make requests and decisions under the Children and Families Act 2014 applies to them directly, rather than to their parents. Parents, or other family members, can continue to support young people in making decisions, or act on their behalf, provided that the young person is happy for them to do so, and it is likely that parents will remain closely involved in the great majority of cases.
>
> (SEND Code of Practice, 2015, 8.13, p. 126)

Maintaining a balance between the wishes of parents and of the pupil may be tricky for schools, and again preparation is the key to success. Potential difficulties will be kept to a minimum when throughout the schooling parents have been used to their child being consulted.

Annual review meetings

Annual reviews can be an ordeal for pupils, parents and professionals alike. It takes time to help a pupil with SEND to develop the ability to 'speak his or her mind', without putting words into their mouths. It is not enough for them to be called into a meeting for five minutes and be asked a few questions before being sent back to class. Pupils have to be prepared over a long period of time: first to become used to talking about how they feel and what they think about school, second to begin to believe that what they say actually matters to adults, and that action will be taken based on their views. A number of questions such as below, prepared in advance of the meeting, will enable the pupil to talk through them with an adult and have the answers jotted down.

- What do you like about school?
- What do you feel proud of?
- Who are your friends?
- What do you want to learn to do better?
- Are you worried about anything to do with school?
- Do you join any clubs or activities after school? Tell me about it.
- What do you look forward to doing in the next year?

The pupil comments form can be used to record a pupil's answers and can be presented to the meeting (see Figure 7.3).

Some pupils will not feel able, or will choose not to attend the meeting in person, but they must always be given the option of attending. If the pupil is not present, his or her responses to the pre-prepared questions must be presented and shared at the meeting. Alternatively, a video link may be set up in a room nearby, through which the pupil can be asked questions. Even in situations where the pupil does not want to, or cannot take part in the meeting, a one-page profile completed by the student can be given to each adult. This would help to focus attention on the child's aspirations, his or her likes and dislikes, and preferred methods of support. (A proforma for a one-page profile can be found in Figure 1.2 on p. 14.)

The voice of the pupil with no verbal communication

Some pupils with SEND do not have verbal communication, and so will be unable to contribute their views in conventional ways. No matter what their degree of SEND, it is even more important for these pupils to participate in decisions affecting their lives. Sometimes it is assumed that it is not possible for pupils with no verbal communication to formulate opinions, and that their participation is not feasible. In order to hear that 'inner voice' it will be necessary for the adults involved to know the pupil well, as communication might be through signing, facial expression, gesture or behaviour.

It is not always straightforward to work out how much a pupil understands. Some pupils with SEND have good expressive language, but poor comprehension. For example, pupils with Williams syndrome speak well with an apparently good vocabulary, but their understanding of spoken language is significantly delayed. Presumptions we make about a child's level of understanding may not be accurate. He or she may understand much less than we think, and need much more preparation and visual support; or, as with James in the following case study, he or she may understand a great deal more.

Name:	Class/Year group:

What I enjoy in school:

What I have achieved:

What I want to do better:

The clubs and activities I do at school:

What I look forward to doing next year:

Signed _____ (pupil)

Signed _____ (tutor)

Figure 7.3 Pupil comments form

© 2016 *Meeting Special Educational Needs in Secondary Classrooms*, Sue Briggs, Routledge

Case study: James

James lived in the north-west of England. In 1974 he was 12 years old and a pupil at a school for children who were 'severely subnormal', as the school was then designated. James had cerebral palsy and he had minimal voluntary control over his body. He had no verbal communication and limited facial expression. He spent seven hours a day, five days a week, either sitting in a red plastic wheelchair or lying on a beanbag. He was in the school's special care class for secondary age pupils. Each morning he was bathed and had a session with the physiotherapist. He spent the rest of the day watching a mobile, listening to music or being fed.

In 1975 James was given a very basic electronic communication aid that he was taught to control by using a head pointer. This was the first skill that James had ever been taught. In fact, James picked up the skills so quickly that he was soon communicating spontaneously and the adults around him realised that while he was disabled physically, his only intellectual impairment was his lack of education.

In order to hear the voice of pupils like James, with profound and complex SEND, teachers need to take time to observe how the pupil responds. Responses may include the direction of gaze, or turning the body towards or away from a stimulus. The pupil might nod or shake the head as options are shown, or in response to questions with a yes/no answer. He or she may reach out and grasp objects and people, or push them away. Responses such as smiles, tears and laughter will give pointers as to how a pupil feels about different situations and people.

When the concepts involved are too intellectually challenging, pupils may genuinely be unable to express their opinions about their own future. For this they should be encouraged to make choices about day-to-day events: the kind of drink they would like; the music they want to listen to; who they want to spend time with, etc. This day-to-day decision making is vital if pupils are not to remain totally dependent on adults throughout life.

Practical strategies

The following are practical suggestions for eliciting the voice of the pupil with SEND. There can be no guarantee that the strategies will work for a particular pupil. Try several approaches, or adapt them to fit the needs of your pupils.

Questionnaires

Questionnaires are a very useful way of gauging how a pupil feels about issues in school. A combination of words, symbols, pictures and photographs will support understanding, and responses may be gauged using simply drawn faces showing different emotions. (A symbol questionnaire in Figure 7.4 follows.)

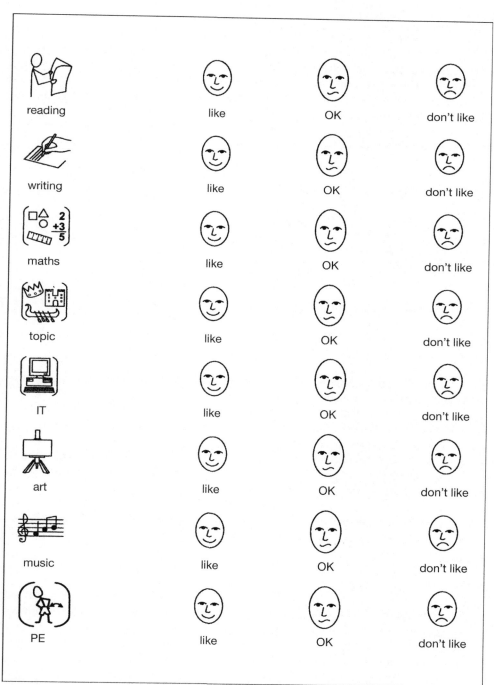

reading	like	OK	don't like
writing	like	OK	don't like
maths	like	OK	don't like
topic	like	OK	don't like
IT	like	OK	don't like
art	like	OK	don't like
music	like	OK	don't like
PE	like	OK	don't like

Figure 7.4 Symbol questionnaire

Smiley faces

Simple line drawings showing different facial expressions can be enormously useful in gauging a pupil's feelings about aspects of school. Happy and sad face cards or posters will give most pupils a way of telling how they feel just by pointing, touching or turning towards one of the faces. Software such as Clicker 6 enables the faces to be displayed side by side on a computer screen. A mouse click or a touch monitor is used to select the face that matches how the pupil feels. The level of complexity can be increased by adding additional faces showing a range of different expressions, but the meaning of these additional faces will need to be taught before they are used.

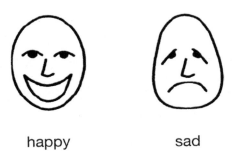

happy   sad

Signing

For some pupils with SEND, signing is the primary mode of expressive communication. Adults and/or other pupils who support the pupil with SEND to give his or her views must be able to sign – and understand signs – at the same level as or better than the pupil. To be able to draw out a pupil's precise meaning it may be necessary to involve a more expert signing communicator. This resource may be especially important for pupils with SEND who are rarely precise signers themselves. Their signs have to be read in conjunction with context, vocalisations, facial expression and other gestures. An adult who knows the pupil and regularly communicates by sign with him or her, is the ideal person to translate the child's wishes. Where no expert signer is available, a combination of signing and symbols, pictures or photographs is more likely to be successful than reliance on signing alone.

Symbols

Symbols have two distinct uses in supporting pupils to give their views. First, they can be used with or instead of text, to enable the pupil to understand information and questions. Second, they can be used to give the pupil a means of letting other people know what they want. This might be through touching or pointing to symbols, sequencing them into sentences, or putting preferences into priority order. Communication cards with a simple format can be tailored to match the ability of individual pupils and situations, from two choices, to a grid containing over a hundred symbols that can be combined to give complex and precise responses instead of or in addition to speech. Symbol choice or preference sheets can be made very easily, and pupils can colour in the different options using one colour to show they like the option, and another if they dislike the option.

Traffic lights

All children are familiar with traffic lights and their meanings. A paper model of traffic lights is a fun way for a pupil to say how they feel about situations in simple terms. The pupil responds to questions by pointing to or touching the requisite colour – green if they are happy for a situation to continue, amber if they are unsure or just not too keen, and red if they definitely want the situation to stop. The colours can also be on removable cards that the pupil can lift up and put on to a representative object or picture. A traffic lights template (Figure 7.5) follows.

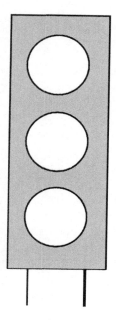

Figure 7.5 Traffic lights template

Draw and write

'Draw and write' is a technique where the pupil draws a person or an object, is then asked to talk about what they have drawn, and the pupil or an adult writes the words around the picture. Pupils can be asked, for example, to draw things or people that make them happy or frightened in school. When the pupil is comfortable with the technique, the questions can be extended to encourage self-reflection, such as 'What do you do that makes teachers feel pleased?' Drawing at the same time as speaking has the added advantage of slowing adults down, making them easier to understand. Both the adult and the pupil draw as they speak. No artistic skills are required, as stick figures are used for people and basic representations for everything else. Speech or thoughts can be recorded in bubbles coming from the figures, and colours may be added to show different emotions. A focus on the drawing also minimises eye contact during the conversations, which some pupils with SEND can find threatening. In the example below, Shane has drawn himself outside in what is for him a very scary situation – being confronted by barking dogs.

'Draw and write' takes the focus away from the other person's face and adds a visual component to spoken interactions. By asking the pupil to draw first the control of the ensuing discussion remains with the child, and so increases the likelihood that his or her opinions are heard. This is preferable to responding to questions solely from the adult's agenda. 'Draw and write' also creates a paper document that can be shared in meetings. The following is an example of the 'draw and write' technique, by Christopher, Year 7, 'What do you do to make people happy?'

Cue cards

Cue cards (see Figure 7.6) can be used to encourage children to talk more fully about school-related events that have happened in the recent past. The cards can contain words, for example, first I . . ., then I . . ., in the end I . . ., etc., or symbols, such as a stick figure for people, a tree to represent the world outside, or faces to represent feelings. The cards help pupils to structure their thinking and narrative with only minimal questioning by the adult. They can act as prompts for ideas about people, talk, settings, feelings and consequences. When practised in the use of the cue cards, pupils are able to retell incidents or a series of events and correctly include significant detail.

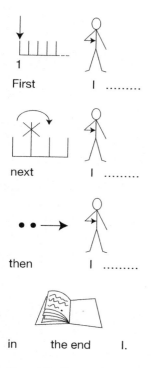

First   I   ....

next   I   ....

then   I   ....

in   the end   I.

Figure 7.6 Cue cards

Mat techniques

Some pupils with SEND need a larger format with which to make choices. Mat techniques involve a pupil moving their whole body to specific mats to show preferences. Mat techniques are also especially useful for pupils who have limited fine motor skills, but who can move by walking, crawling or shuffling.

Plain mats are placed on the floor (PE mats or carpet samples are ideal). On to these mats are then stuck numbers, words, photographs, symbols or pictures, showing different facial expressions. The pupil responds to a question by moving to the mat that represents his or her choice. If you are unsure whether the pupil meant to choose a particular mat, or whether they went to the wrong one by mistake, you could try the mats set further apart, sometimes even into the four corners of the room. In this way the choice is more definite, and the pupil can return to the centre of the room before making the next decision.

Speech and thought bubbles

Coming from a photograph or a drawing of the pupil him- or herself, speech and thought bubbles can be used to record responses. Sometimes seeing themselves from outside – as in a photograph or a drawing – helps a pupil to reflect on a situation more objectively. 'Me' bubbles with labels such as 'I can', 'I like', 'I am going to', 'I want', 'I don't like', etc., give a focus to questions (see Figures 7.7a and 7.7b).

By focusing initially on positive feelings and then moving gradually to more negative statements, the overall response is balanced, and any negative feelings do not crowd out the positive responses.

Masks

The use of masks can help a pupil to talk about feelings, literally from behind a mask. The mask may make a pupil feel more confident to talk about school and his or her priorities. Masks can be bought from educational suppliers but are much better if made with and by the pupil who can then decide which emotion a mask should show. Plain masks can be bought, but paper plates are much cheaper and just as effective. Using the masks in role-play enables situations that pupils find difficult to be rehearsed, and different, more appropriate resolutions will be found. Pupils who do not like to wear masks, or who have limited speech, can be asked to choose a mask that shows how they feel about a particular situation.

Gauging strength of feeling

Where a teacher needs to gauge the depth of a pupil's feelings about a situation, a visual and/or tactile strategy will give a more accurate measure than words alone. There are several ways this can be done, such as:

* Invite the pupil to award him- or herself a number of sticky stars – this is often an accurate measure of the child or young person's self-esteem.
* Squeeze toothpaste from a tube with the amount squeezed showing stronger or weaker feelings.
* Unroll a ball of string or ribbon.
* Put dried beans or marbles into a pot – the more beans the stronger the feeling.

A ladder laid down on the floor gives pupils a physical way of showing how strongly they feel about situations, and/or how much they care. Put large numbers from one to ten between each of the rungs of the ladder. The pupil is then asked a question and is asked to show, by moving along a number of rungs, how much they do or do not want something to happen, or how much they do or do not like something or someone.

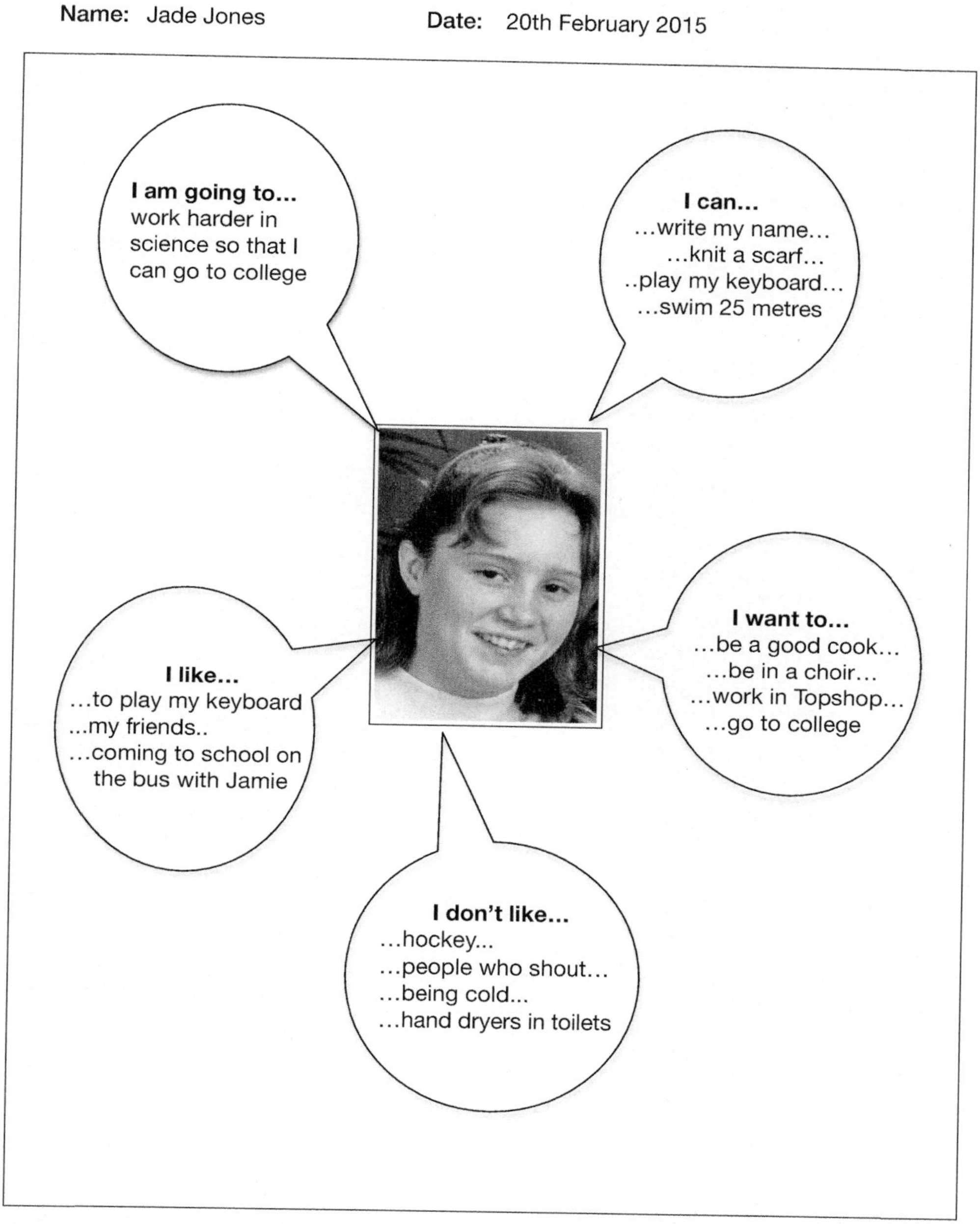

Name: Jade Jones   **Date:** 20th February 2015

I am going to... work harder in science so that I can go to college

I can... ...write my name... ...knit a scarf... ..play my keyboard... ...swim 25 metres

I like... ...to play my keyboard ...my friends.. ...coming to school on the bus with Jamie

I want to... ...be a good cook... ...be in a choir... ...work in Topshop... ...go to college

I don't like... ...hockey... ...people who shout... ...being cold... ...hand dryers in toilets

Figure 7.7a 'Me' bubbles

Name: **Date:**

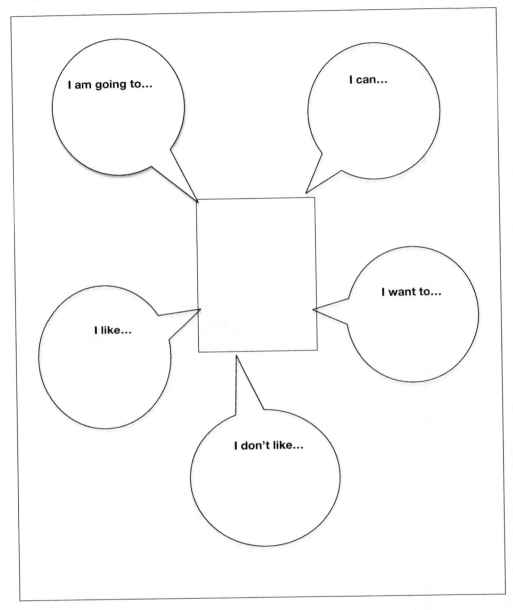

Figure 7.7b Template for 'me' bubbles

© 2016 *Meeting Special Educational Needs in Secondary Classrooms*, Sue Briggs, Routledge

Concept maps

Concept maps can be used to help a pupil formulate their ideas by creating a visual plan. Words, pictures, photographs, symbols and different colours can be used to reflect a child's feelings and wishes accurately. Pupils with SEND often have problems visualising abstract concepts, and concept maps make their ideas more concrete. Balancing the pros and cons of a decision is made easier in the form of a concept map, and is supported by the addition of colours, symbols and pictures.

Self books and films

An opportunity to be the star of one's own story can have a big influence on a pupil's self-esteem. Start with photographs of the pupil in different everyday situations. The pupil then dictates a narrative based on the photographs. Other photographs might be included of people at home and at school so as to give a more rounded portrayal of the pupil's life. Other books may be created to support the pupil through times of change, and to help him or her make decisions. For example, a booklet on each of the different courses available for study in Key Stage 4 will give the pupil important information, and he or she can indicate their preferences by handing over the requisite booklet.

By creating stories about imaginary children who experience similar problems to their own, pupils with SEND can in a safe setting be helped to find solutions, and explore alternative strategies. The fictional context adds objectivity to familiar situations and events, and the story can be re-read as necessary. Reading about events in the third person helps some pupils to talk through the problems they experience when talking directly about themselves.

A short film of the pupil can be made in a similar way to the 'self' books using a camera or old mobile phone. If videos are to be taken of pupils, parents and carers must be informed and their permission sought.

Posters

A larger-scale format is more appropriate for some pupils. With the pupil, create a poster showing aspects of their life with key words or symbols and 'feelings', and written in different colours to show how the pupil feels about each aspect. As with concept maps, the poster by using arrows or coloured lines makes it possible to link ideas and feelings visually. Thought and speech bubbles may be added to show the pupil's own words.

Poems

Poetry creates unique emotional and conceptual opportunities because by utilising individual words and short phrases it frees pupils with SEND from the constraints of sentence construction. Start by giving the pupil an object or a picture to hold. The pupil then dictates words and phrases relating to the object or picture, starting with descriptive words and then moving to more emotional language. Acrostics are a good starting point, as the initial sounds give phonic prompts such as in the poem below by Josef, writing about his friends. This poem says a great deal about how Josef feels about his friends in general and David in particular. David has behavioural, social and emotional difficulties, and was not considered by Josef's teacher to be one of his friends, but just one of several boys on Josef's lunch table. It turned out that while Josef liked swapping sandwiches, he often ended up with the other boys' rejects, and so lunchtime supervisors kept a closer eye on the table.

'Friends' by Josef

F – fun
R – reading partner
I – in school
E – English bulldogs
N – naughty sometimes
D – David
S – sandwich swap

Facial expression photographs and drawings

Facial expression photographs are available from several educational resource suppliers, but they are very expensive. A more cost-effective alternative is to make your own set for the school using a camera. Either the pupil with SEND is photographed making different facial expressions, and/or other pupils are involved. This makes an excellent project for GCSE drama students, with results as good as anything that can be purchased. Laminating the photographs will protect them from damage so they may be used over and over again.

Drama, role play and dance

Drama and role play with people they trust offer pupils with SEND the opportunity to work through and rehearse situations and emotions. Drama broadens a pupil's range of emotional expression, incorporates facial expression, movement, and words, and allows pupils to practise different ways of interacting with other people. In the same way, dance introduces pupils to an additional medium of communication by developing new body shapes, gestures and whole-body movements. Through drama or dance pupils with limited verbal communication may be able to communicate how they feel much more effectively and creatively.

Role play is a very powerful medium and can help pupils with SEND to practise different and more appropriate responses to situations they find difficult. Some caution may need to be exercised, as a pupil may become distressed at reliving situations they find painful or uncomfortable.

Summary

Hearing and listening to the voice of the pupil with SEND will take time and effort. Take the trouble to hear what they have to say, by whatever means, and that communication will always be worthwhile. People with SEND know what they want from life, and those aspirations are much like those of everyone else – to be loved, to be safe, to have a home and a family, to be respected. If one of the strategies in this chapter does not work, try another, and another, and keep on trying. As with James in the case study, there is always much more to the pupil with SEND than you ever could have expected.

Chapter 8 looks at the challenges and opportunities of transitions.

Transitions
Inclusion challenges and opportunities

Thorough preparation for inclusion is the most important factor for success, both to prepare for greater diversity in your school and to include a welcome for pupils with SEND. The time from a first impression through to the child arriving on the first day of a new school year is the window of opportunity. Use this opportunity to find out as much as possible about the child and what the school can do to make the placement a success. The preparation, liaison and training undertaken will be of enormous value for the future development of the school, and will 'clear the ramp'– as in the Michael Giangreco illustration in Chapter 1 – for other pupils with a more diverse range of needs and talents. Times of change and transition are potentially stressful periods for all children. For children with SEND stress is often significant. Not all children will have difficulties with transitions, and so some may not need additional support. The trouble is that we don't know beforehand which children will find it hard, or which situation will spark off anxiety – and we should anticipate and plan for transitions however a child may have reacted in the past.

The moves from primary to secondary school, and from secondary school into further or higher education, training or work, are some of the more significant periods of transition in anyone's life. The majority of children and young people manage these transitions with some trepidation, but also with excitement at the new experiences ahead of them. Many pupils with SEND will share this excitement and look forward to the new challenges ahead. But there are other pupils with SEND who will experience extreme anxiety, and who will need careful planning and support both to guide them through transitions, and to enable schools, colleges and training providers to make the necessary adjustments to equipment, systems and practices. This chapter examines these aspects of transition.

Preparing for transitions

Successful transitions do not just happen – it is no good 'waiting to see how he fits in' because the probability is that 'he' won't! When the child's behaviour becomes inappropriate or challenging because he or she is anxious, the child will get the blame. If the school has not made reasonable adjustments for the transition or change, it is not the child's fault if the situation breaks down – as in the following case study about George.

The time commitment necessary to plan transitions for pupils with SEND may seem burdensome to SENCOs and teachers, but time spent developing a robust strategy to support a pupil before, through and after a move to another school, will save disruption to other children and will avoid many hours of future work writing behaviour plans, meeting with educational psychologists, talking to parents, and so on.

Case study: George

George was a very able boy with Asperger's syndrome who had progressed successfully through his primary school and who achieved well above national expectations in tests at the end of Key Stage 2. His Year 6 teacher and the primary school SENCO invested a great deal of time and attention in liaising with the secondary school to plan his transfer into Year 7. A transition plan was written at the start of Year 6 and George and his family made several visits to the nearby high school both in and out of school time. A teaching assistant to support George in his new school was assigned during the previous spring term and she spent two days each week with him in the primary school in the summer term to get to know George and what support he needed to learn well. The secondary school believed that this was enough preparation for George to make a successful transfer to his new school. All appeared to be going swimmingly.

The situation began to unravel when the assigned TA's husband got a new job abroad over the summer holidays and she resigned. No one thought to tell George and his family. Even though a new TA was recruited in time for the start of term, on his first day in the secondary school George was met by a complete stranger to him. Despite the efforts of his primary school and the previous TA, other than the SENCO no member of the secondary school teaching staff had any information or understanding of the difficulties that George might face in the first few weeks in his new school. As he had full-time one-to-one support, his teachers relinquished any responsibility for George's learning or behaviour and expected his TA to make the lessons accessible for him.

George found the situation intolerable. His new TA stayed physically very close to him and constantly spoke to him in lessons. He found it impossible to focus on both the teacher and his TA, even though he found the academic work very easy. His parents contacted the SENCO to let him know that George had become reluctant to get out of bed and unwilling to go to school. A meeting was arranged for the following week. However, the following day George's anxiety boiled over and he hit out at the TA during a lesson, bruising her arm. He was immediately given a permanent exclusion, which was the school policy when a pupil was violent towards a member of staff. Even though the school governors overturned this decision some weeks later, George and his parents were no longer willing for him to return to the school. He had lasted only eight weeks. As a result of this mishandling of the transition process, George ended up in a special school for children with ASD many miles away from his home.

Whether the plan is for a big change, such as the move from primary to secondary, or simply a change from one lesson or activity to another, it should be planned in some detail, and the child pre-warned and prepared. Create the plan with the child's parents and other members of the Year 7 team. This ensures that everyone working with the pupil knows and understands his or her strengths and needs, and boosts confidence that the pupil can be supported through the transition to a successful long-term placement. This confidence is especially important when a pupil has in the past had difficulties with change and transition, which understandably may make staff feel apprehensive.

As was stated in Chapter 1, the Children and Families Act 2014 secures a general presumption in law of mainstream education in relation to decisions about where children and young people with SEN should be educated; the Equality Act 2010 provides protection from discrimination for disabled people. The SEND Code of Practice 2015 (1.27, p. 26) states that schools and admissions authorities:

- *must not* refuse to admit a child who has SEN but does not have an EHC plan because they do not feel able to cater for those needs;
- *must not* refuse to admit a child on the grounds that they do not have an EHC plan.

It is understandable for secondary schools to have concerns around admitting pupils with SEND, especially those pupils who may already be known to have emotional, social and mental health difficulties, and about their potential impact on other pupils.

Mainstream placements for children with SEND frequently break down at the transition from primary to secondary school. This might be because the child's parents feel the secondary school is not an appropriate place for their child, or that the teachers in the primary school may believe that a move to a special school would be better for the child. There are many concerns voiced such as:

- *The child wouldn't 'cope' in a mainstream secondary school.* It is not up to the child with SEND to 'cope' in the secondary school. It is the responsibility of the school to change to meet the needs of a more diverse population of children, and to give the child the necessary support to be able to succeed.
- *The secondary school curriculum is not appropriate for a child with SEND.* The school's own accessibility plan and SEN Information Report must identify how the curriculum is to be made accessible for all children. By using a little creativity and teamwork, the curriculum in any school can be adapted to meet the needs of children with SEND and in the process the curriculum will be better and the more accessible for *all* pupils.
- *The child does not have the personal organisation to be able to move from class to class after each lesson.* There are many children who struggle for the first few weeks to find their way around a large school, but eventually they become familiar with the layout of the site and settle to the new system. It may take a little longer for children with SEND, but with support from adults and other pupils they too will learn the routine. Some secondary schools organise Year 7 in a 'home room' model, where the children stay in their classroom base for most subjects, but go out for some lessons such as science in the laboratories and PE in the gym. Over the course of Year 7 more and more lessons are taken away from the base, until by the start of Year 8 the children have the confidence and skills to move from class to class.
- *The child would be bullied.* This is a major concern for parents and teachers alike. But what kind of communities are our secondary schools if we are afraid to send children there? Schools must have robust anti-bullying policies, and to keep them safe should support any vulnerable pupils. Often the perception and fear of bullying is much greater than the reality, and most children with special educational needs are happy and safe in their schools. For schools really to be safe and pleasant places, we ought to work towards inclusion so that we create safe and welcoming school environments for every child.
- *Secondary school teachers only teach their subjects, they aren't SEN teachers.* All teachers are teachers of children with special educational needs no matter in which phase they

work or which subject they teach. All teachers who have trained in the past twenty years should expect to teach pupils with a diverse range of abilities and needs in all their classes, and to adapt their teaching strategies for and to them.

- *The child would not have a peer group.* Children who have been included successfully into a mainstream primary school already have a peer group with which to move up to the secondary school. Good schools (that foster respect for diversity and celebrate all achievement) will encourage that peer group to be maintained into adolescence. It is positive for children with SEND to meet other people who are disabled, or who have a similar kind of learning difficulty, but this will happen through parent support groups or clubs in the evening.
- *Children at the special school can stay there until they are 19.* An important part of growing and maturing is having the opportunity to experience new situations and new people. At age 16 most young people with SEND are ready for a different style of educational experience. The transfer to further education should be seen as a positive step, especially as local further education colleges offer a range of courses to meet the needs of young people of all abilities. These courses allow and include a continued focus on basic literacy, numeracy and life skills. In addition, the young people learn new skills that prepare them for the world of work.

The parents of children with SEND do have a right to opt for a mainstream secondary school, and often children with SEND go on to have happy and successful secondary school experiences – but only where the school has prepared effectively to include these children. This preparation will include:

- Development of a rigorous inclusive ethos among governors, senior leaders and all teaching and support staff.
- Recruitment of a trained and knowledgeable SENCO who is a member of the school leadership team and who has the skills and status to have strategic oversight of the budget and provision for SEND, and the impact of that provision. The SENCO must be able to offer support to staff, but also to hold to account any member of staff whose practice is less than good.
- Identification of a budget for SEND that includes funding to enable teachers to take the time necessary to work effectively with the families of pupils with SEND (see Chapter 3).
- Training for staff on effective practice for pupils with SEND including training on any specific area of SEND of current or prospective pupils.
- Provision of appropriate equipment and resources.
- Rigorous systems of liaison with feeder primary schools and with local colleges of further education, training providers, and employers.

Welcoming pupils with SEND to your school

We all need to feel wanted, whether that is being made to feel welcome when we move to a new area, attend a church for the first time, join a club, or just when buying a paper from the newsagents. How we are made to feel welcome can be difficult to pinpoint, but it is that initial positive contact that makes us want to return. As teachers, we get only one chance to make that first impression in extending a warm welcome to pupils.

When a group of pupils were asked what made them feel welcome, their answers were refreshing and simple:

- 'A smile.'
- 'A handshake.'
- 'They treat me as if they like me.'
- 'Someone to show me where to go.'
- 'When someone spends time with me.'

These responses give clues about what makes people feel welcome when they visit schools and how that welcome can be achieved.

All schools aim to be open and welcoming and most spend time and resources to create a positive first impression. Within such a busy environment it can be difficult to maintain a consistent level of welcome. Parents who arrive by appointment at 10 a.m., when everyone is in class, are likely to get the full works – smiles from the administration staff, a warm greeting, the offer of coffee, comfortable chairs on which to wait, information about the school to read, and a prompt response from the member of staff concerned. However, if parents were to arrive at 2.30 p.m. and during a lesson change on the day of the school play, would the welcome be the same?

The first welcome into the secondary school is so important for children with SEND and their parents or carers. By the time children reach this transition stage they will probably have experienced rejection and discrimination on many occasions. Some parents feel they have had to battle every step of the way for their child, and see schools and local authorities as obstacles in their fight for the right provision for their child. To be made to feel welcome as they walk through the door gives a really good basis in starting a new school career.

When speaking about transfer to secondary school, the parents' greatest fear is that their child will not be able to cope. When we unpick what parents mean by 'being able to cope', they rarely mean coping with lessons. Parents fear their child will not be able to cope with the apparently chaotic environment which they often see on a first visit to the school. A most effective way to test the first impressions given by your school is to ask governors and teachers from other schools to visit unannounced at different times within a week – a sort of 'mystery shopper' exercise. The experiences can be fed back to the whole staff and any areas for development may then be addressed.

The reality is that parents have the right to choose a mainstream secondary school placement for their child. The choice, and the transition from the primary school, will prove more successful with a positive joint approach from both schools.

Working with primary schools to improve transitions for pupils with SEND

Liaison with feeder primary schools to secure smooth transitions from Year 6 to Year 7 is an important aspect of the secondary school's responsibilities, both in terms of general forward planning, and in terms of potential pupils with special needs. Where there are good relationships with feeder primary schools (and regular meetings are held throughout the year), secondary schools will have a sound knowledge of potential pupils several years in advance. This means that many issues, such as staff training, access, or SEN provision, can be addressed in good time for when the pupil arrives. A teacher must be assigned to lead the liaison with the primary school. To be sure of success this liaison should be led by a member of the secondary school leadership team supported, for pupils with SEND, by the SENCO. Year 7 tutors would also be valuable members of the transition team, especially as they will eventually be the form tutor for the pupil or pupils with SEND.

Transition from primary school for pupils with Education, Health and Care plans

Because this transition is such a major event in the life of a child with more significant SEND, planning should begin at least two years before the move to secondary school. The liaison should have begun well before the Year 5 annual review of a child's EHC plan and this meeting should always have the pupil's transition to secondary school as the main focus. This review is of critical importance, and representatives from all potential secondary schools should always attend. This is because decisions made at the transition review will shape a pupil's secondary education and will determine their future life opportunities. It is worth attending even if you are unsure whether or not the child will move to your school. This meeting must be attended by:

- the child – he or she must be present for at least part of the annual review and his/her views captured beforehand in some way, on paper or in a video or audio recording;
- the parents or main care-givers;
- any key worker or supporter invited by the parents
- the child's class teacher;
- support staff who work closely with the child;
- the headteacher or the primary school SENCO;
- the SENCOs or other representatives from local secondary schools;
- key professionals from other agencies, depending on a child's needs: educational psychologist, speech and language therapist, physiotherapist, occupation therapist, learning support service teacher – whoever is professionally involved with the child.

This review is often the parents' and child's first contact with anyone from a secondary school, so do try to be as positive as possible about including the child in your school. Parents will be alert to any even vaguely negative comments or doubts that are expressed – and there is no need to concern parents at this early stage. This means that even if you have grave concerns about including in your school a child with particular needs, you must not use those concerns to put parents off, such as suggesting that they look at another school with more facilities or a special school. Rejoice that parents have chosen to send their child to your school – you have over a year to plan to get it right.

The meeting must focus on the child and parents' aspirations for the future and the outcomes they want for their child from the next two or three years. This gives the secondary school a positive course of action on which to base the planning for any necessary amendments in terms of physical or curriculum access, and which will enable the primary school and parents to prepare the child for the transition.

The most important decision for the annual review meeting to make is 'who will co-ordinate the transition'. This must be one person based in the primary school who takes on the responsibility for liaising between the schools and the parents. Without this close liaison and co-ordination, some children will fall 'between the planks'.

Pupil involvement

All children must be involved in the transition planning process and the more involved the child, the greater the chance of success. The child will feel more confident when working through the transition *with* others, rather than *by* others being propelled into a new situation. Tell the child about impending changes and make it into an exciting adventure. Create picture books about the new situation using photographs of the child acting out what he or she will do and how they will feel in the new setting or after the change.

Case study: Ayesha

Ayesha transferred from her primary school to the secondary school on the same site. During Year 6 her behaviour deteriorated significantly as she become more and more anxious about the move to the new school, even though it was just next door. Ayesha's parents, her class teacher and the SENCO from the secondary school met to decide how to support her through the transition and how to lessen her anxiety. A week after the meeting Ayesha and a teaching assistant visited the secondary school. They were given a tour of the campus and Ayesha was photographed in different key parts of the school – the science laboratory, the sports hall, the canteen, the library. These photographs were then put into a book and Ayesha wrote sentences underneath about what she had seen. She took the book home to share with her family, and added other pictures and information about the school from the school website and SEN Information Report. During the visit Ayesha was told that she would be able to join lunchtime and after-school sports clubs. She was delighted about this because she had a real talent for and love of running. These clubs became a focus for Ayesha throughout the transition, and she began to see the positive aspects of the new school and to look forward to going there.

Preparatory visits

Parental visits

In the months before a decision needs to be made about a secondary school, or in the time leading up to the Year 5 transition review for those pupils with EHC plans, it is imperative that parents/carers of children with SEND are supported to visit numerous schools. If parents have visited all potential schools, they will be able to make an informed choice based on their knowledge of the child and what they, the parents/carers, want from the school.

Most parents of children with an identified SEND choose to send their child to the local secondary school. This allows the child to maintain his or her friendship groups and to be part of the local community, and fosters opportunities for contacts with other children outside school. Parents are likely to feel very anxious at this first visit and will be just as interested in the school atmosphere and environment as in the Ofsted report. But like other parents, parents of children with SEND will be interested in the Ofsted report too, because they also want their child to go to a school that is good or outstanding.

This first visit by parents is crucial to the future success of the placement, and it is best if on this occasion parents visit without their child. They can then the better observe and ask about the school without worrying about the child's reaction to new surroundings, and they are the more able to discuss freely with the teacher their hopes and concerns. Build in time to talk to new parents individually, find out about their child, and give information about the learning activities and the school's expectations.

Implied negatives

When parents of children with special needs visit a prospective school for their child, they will be very sensitive to the responses of the headteacher and other staff members. It does not need to be the blunt: 'Oh, I don't think we could meet those needs in this school.' Parents all too often report that headteachers or SENCOs recommend that they visit a particular special school or a school with a resourced provision or 'unit', implying that a different school would be a better placement for the pupil.

The negative is often more subtle, however:

'We have a very high proportion of more able pupils in our school.'

'We expect all our pupils to pass five or more GCSEs.'

'Do you think your daughter could cope in this school?'

These may be valid points about the school, but saying such things may make the parent/carer of a child with special needs feel their child will be unwelcome.

Schools should give parents information about the school's special needs provision, the pastoral support that is available, or even the merits of the drama department. Identifying these aspects will help parents leave the school with positive feelings and provide the basis for them to make an informed decision.

Pupil visits

If a pupil is to have a successful long-term placement, getting to know a secondary school well before transfer is very important. This is most easily achieved by arranging additional preparatory visits throughout the couple of terms pre-transfer. Obviously, these visits can take place only where a secondary placement has been agreed well in advance. The importance of thinking well ahead cannot be over-emphasised. Where a child has an EHC plan ideally parents will need to have chosen a school before the Year 5 transition review if there is to be time for preparatory visits to be arranged.

Where secondary schools have effective liaison and regular contact with their feeder primaries, the process will be much simpler. Pupils will be used to visiting the 'big school' as part of usual practice. But even where primary and secondary schools share a campus, that contact can sometimes be merely superficial.

It may take some children up to two years to settle fully into a new school. This is particularly the case where they transfer from a small primary school to a large secondary. Even pupils without SEND often find it hard to fit into the new community, with its written – and unwritten – rules and new social norms. Merely moving from one class to another, through busy corridors, carrying all the equipment they need for that day, is daunting for many children.

The first visit

Ideally, the visits need to start early in the autumn term, with a joint visit for pupil and parents/carers after other pupils have left at the end of the school day. Coming to terms with the size and layout of the buildings is very helpful before having to deal with the social demands of the school. Schools can suggest to parents/carers that they or their child take photographs of different areas of the school during the visit. This gives the child opportunities at home to look at the photographs and ask questions. The family can make a scrapbook about the school to which the child can add after each visit. On this first visit a key worker or mentor should be assigned to the pupil. The key worker will be the parent/carer's first point of contact, and will be responsible for monitoring the transition, and supporting the pupil's social and academic progress through the school.

The second joint visit

This second visit should follow within three or four weeks of the first visit, and should take place during the school day. This visit should be unhurried, with plenty of opportunities for all to ask questions. The child should not be expected to take part in any activities at this stage. A prospective pupil will best be left to watch and absorb the atmosphere in the security of their parents' company. Any access issues may be discussed at this visit, giving the school plenty of time to make the necessary reasonable adjustments.

Open day

The family could visit again for the school open day or evening. This will give them the opportunity to meet other parents, and the child to meet potential future classmates. These open days often include family activities based on the secondary curriculum and these are an ideal introduction for a pupil with SEND to experience learning in the new setting.

Class visits

An invitation to the child's class to visit the secondary school for an art day, or a Christmas concert, will create positive associations without singling out the pupil with special needs. Concert programmes or completed art work could be added to the scrapbook started after the first visit.

Small group visits

In the spring term the links with the pupil's class can be developed further, and small group visits for specific lessons arranged. The pupil with special needs, along with two friends and a teaching assistant could join Year 7 classes for music or drama, depending on individual particular interests. Photographs, completed worksheets or play scripts could again be added to the scrapbook, building up the information on the school and increasing confidence.

Joining Year 7 lessons

In the summer term, regular weekly visits will need to take place. These visits should include time spent with classes in the library, science laboratories, design and technology workshop, and the gym. Some of these visits should be for the pupil and a teaching assistant, some for small groups, and some for the whole year group. Information about safety in these specialist areas can be included in the scrapbook so that the pupil is prepared for the start of the new school year.

Uniform

An exciting part of the move to a new school is having new clothes or a uniform to wear. Encourage the pupil with SEND to wear the school jumper or blazer when visiting the school. During the transition period this will help him or her feel more grown up and a part of the school community.

The form or tutor room

Before the end of the summer term the pupil should be shown the new form room and given a place to keep his or her personal belongings – a drawer or a box in a cupboard containing a few personal items from home, a favourite book, drawing paper and pens – that is, anything that will be familiar and recognisable when the pupil starts at the school after the summer holiday.

A video of the school

A short video of a school day will give the pupil something to watch during the summer holiday and prepare for the transition. The video will start the pupil and his or her family talking about the new school, and will build awareness and realistic expectations of how that secondary school operates.

Time spent preparing for transition from primary to secondary is never wasted, and the more comfortable and confident the child feels about the school the more successful will be his or her long-term placement.

Case study: Kai

Kai will join Year 7 in September. He has speech and language difficulties and some minor problems with mobility. Kai's mum chose his secondary placement after visiting all the schools in the area. She particularly liked the school because of the welcome she received from the SENCO and how pupils appeared to be happy and confident individuals. Mum,

Kai and his class teacher together made a one-page profile showing what his teachers and other children like and admire about him, what he likes and is good at, and how best to support him. Kai's mum and his teacher also put together a folder of information about Kai – some examples of his art work and writing, a précis of the latest school assessment results and report, and copies of the most recent reports from his therapists. Each time Kai visited the secondary school he was accompanied by the SENCO from the primary school, or his class teacher or teaching assistant. This meant that the secondary school staff had written and verbal information about how to make good provision for Kai based on his personality, his interests and his strengths, as well as his special educational and health needs.

This information, together with the teacher's own observations of Kai, enabled the school to plan adjustments to:

- the curriculum (planning and adapting schemes of work to address Kai's learning needs);
- assessment;
- resources;
- training (signing);
- liaison with the speech and language therapy service;
- the building (an accessible washroom with an adapted toilet) to ensure access for Kai.

Relationships with teachers and support staff

Teachers are hugely influential in the lives of their pupils. As with all relationships, it takes time for staff to build a shared understanding and trust with new students. In that first term helping a new group of children to work as a cohesive group is very important, just as is the content of the subject lessons. All teachers, no matter what their subject specialism, need to get to know and understand the children with SEND in their classes as quickly as possible, because the better the relationship between teacher and pupil, the better the child will learn and behave. This need not take up a great deal of additional time or effort – just make a point of saying hello in the corridor and smile at them!

Where the class or the child is to be supported by a teaching assistant, that TA should also get to know the child before he or she enters the school by making a number of visits to the primary school.

The move to a new school is a major change in a child's life. An additional change of teaching assistant can lead to anxiety and so to inappropriate behaviour. Wherever possible during the term after transition, maintain the pupil's contact with at least one well-known adult from primary school. Some schools have had success by the secondary school employing on a part-time basis the TA who supported the child in primary – just for the first half-term – to work alongside the new TA and to enable the child to settle in the new class.

Additional information for pupils with SEND

In addition to the usual information that schools send to new parents, pupils with SEND will need specific information in preparation for the transition. The most effective way of giving this information is to create a transition pack jointly with the pupil and the primary school. The pack will need to contain the usual information such as school prospectus, uniform details, etc. Possible additional information includes:

- a plan or map of the school campus;
- a short video of the school in action;
- a list of teachers and teaching assistants, with their photographs;
- a symbolic or pictorial timetable;
- a list of the school rules;
- a homework diary.

Much of this information can be included as links to pdf files in the SEN Information Report on the school website.

What do teachers and teaching assistants need to know?

Transition paperwork

The paperwork prepared for transition is key if schools are to have access to detailed information that they need about new pupils with SEND. In order for the transition of pupils with SEND to be successful, the SENCO needs to have as much relevant information as possible in order to make decisions about resources, groupings and support. An example of a completed transition form (Figure 8.1a) follows together with a blank template (Figure 8.1b).

Information for subject teachers

The information given to subject teachers is crucial to a successful placement. Merely to know that a pupil has SEND is insufficient. Teachers require information about a child's particular strengths and needs. However, at the start of a busy term too much information can be a burden, and a one-page profile created with the pupil and his or her parents should be enough to give the important details. The profile should include a photograph of the pupil, his or her interests, any access issues, the pupil's usual mode of communication, support preferences, and any information particular to the subject area, for example, the pupil's speed of changing before PE.

The first day in the new school

If a child has visited the school on several occasions it is useful to ask them to help to show other new pupils around the school. This serves two purposes. First, the pupil will be pleased to be given responsibility and will gain self-esteem. Second, other pupils will have a positive first impression of their classmate with SEND.

Even if the pupil has a teaching assistant assigned to him or her, try not to make the support too overt, especially on that first day. The pupil needs to become used to being independent in the classroom and around the school, and it is best to start as you mean to go on. This is also important in determining how the pupil is perceived by others. All the class will be unsure in the new setting, and if they are encouraged to help each other,

BRADTHORPE ACADEMY

TRANSITION FORM	Name: Katherine Smith	Date of birth: 20/3/2004	Transferring from: St Luke's
	Home address: 8, Bloxham Way, Bradthorpe Tel: 01928 113355 Email: mandpsmith@anymail.co.uk	**Names of parents/carers and siblings:** Mum: Marion Reynolds Dad: Paul Smith Sister: Emily Reynolds (Year 9) Brother: Kyle Smith (Year 3) **Pets:** Dogs – Sheba and Tyson	**Contacts at liaison school:** Mrs Phillips (SENCO) Miss Lewis (Class teacher)

Likes and dislikes: Katherine: I like playing with my friends, dancing and riding my bike. **Recent assessments:** Katherine has a reading age of 8:6. She finds handwriting difficult and uses a tablet for recording her work. **Last book read:** 'The owl who was afraid of the dark' by Jill Tomlinson	**Talents and interests:** Katherine has a lovely singing voice and enjoys all music lessons and activities. She attends Riding for the Disabled classes on Saturdays and can now walk and trot her horse without being led. **Special needs/disability:** Katherine has some physical needs relating to her cerebral palsy. She moves around school using a rear support walking frame but sometimes needs to use a wheelchair. Katherine has some learning difficulties, especially evident in literacy. She works hard and is making good progress as a result of the provision made for her. **Code of Practice: EHC Plan in place**	**Friends:** Narinder and Amy **Preferred mode of communication:** Speech with key word signing. Katherine has good comprehension. **Access:** Rear support walking frame Wheelchair when necessary Tablet computer **Medication:** Anti-convulsant for seizures

Figure 8.1a Example of a completed Year 7 transition form

NAME OF SCHOOL

TRANSITION FORM

	Name:	Date of birth:	Transferring from:
photo	Home address: Tel: Email:	Names of parents/carers and siblings: Pets:	Contacts at liaison school:
Likes and dislikes:	Talents and interests:	Friends: Preferred mode of communication:	
Recent assessments:	Special needs/disability:	Access:	
Last book read:	Code of Practice:	Medication:	

Figure 8.1b Template for transition form

they will quite naturally give support to the pupil with SEND. A planned buddy scheme will ensure this mutual support happens and may be the start of future social groupings.

Pastoral support

Where a key worker or mentor has been assigned to the family in the year before transfer, then that person will already be a familiar face by the time the child starts at the new school. Where a pupil has individual TA support the mentor should be someone other than the child's own teaching assistant. A regular meeting with the pupil once a week should be enough to address any difficulties or misunderstandings that may arise.

Transitions within the school

Any transition has the potential to trigger anxiety, resulting in serious deterioration in self-esteem and behaviour. While we may anticipate that the transfer from primary to secondary school is likely to cause anxiety, other more frequent changes and transitions also have the potential to upset a child's equilibrium. This does not mean that pupils should be sheltered from transitions and change; they need to be prepared for and supported through the transitions. This is not a one-way street, with all the onus on the child to adapt; schools must examine their own situations and systems in order the better to meet individual needs.

Moving from one activity to another

Some pupils with SEND find it difficult to stop one lesson or activity and move on to another, especially if they are involved in a lesson they enjoy, or are not too keen on the one to come. These situations can lead to oppositional behavior and disruption for the whole class. The more a pupil is forced through these transitions the more cemented will become the oppositional behaviours.

The most effective method of avoiding these situations is at the start of each day to prepare the pupil for the day ahead. A symbol schedule or timetable showing the pupil the sequence of activities and lessons throughout the day helps them to understand what

Case study: Fred

Fred found it very hard in the secondary school to get used to the new routine of moving around the school between lessons, and became increasingly anxious as each lesson neared its end. He seemed to become fixated on whatever he was doing and increasingly reluctant to change task. His form tutor collected lesson plans from all Fred's teachers each morning, and created an individual timetable for him at the start of each day that showed not only the subjects but also the activities within each lesson. After each lesson the name of one of Fred's buddies was shown, and this boy helped him to get to the next lesson safely and without incident. The timetable was only necessary for three weeks, after which Fred was able to manage the transitions without this additional support.

is going to happen. For some pupils a more detailed visual timetable will be necessary, especially during the early days following entry to the school, which will help them move between the activities within lessons, in addition to their transition between lessons, as in the case study above.

Assemblies

Assemblies, lunchtimes and other large school gatherings cause some pupils great anxiety and upset, perhaps because of the noise, the larger space in the hall, or just because of the proximity of a large number of people in one place. It is not possible to control this particular environment for a pupil with SEND, but it is possible to give him or her a device to help them cope with the situation. If a pupil finds the hall too noisy, offer an MP3 player with a favourite piece of music or a story to listen to. This blocks out some of the stimuli and gives the pupil some control of what for them is an unpleasant situation.

Symbol timetables and schedules

Symbol timetables or schedules have the advantage of being very flexible, and should there be an unexpected change to the routine, the cards can quickly be rearranged to reflect the new situation. An enjoyable activity for a pupil which can be shared with a teacher, learning mentor or teaching assistant is to create a personal timetable at the start of the day. Pupils are far more motivated to work independently if they have been involved in planning and designing their own timetable. This interactive time can also be used to review the daily routine, discuss changes and reinforce rules.

Generally, schools are not regimented places and often things do not go to plan. With visual support, most children with SEND cope well with the classroom routine, but may have particular difficulties when something they were looking forward to doesn't happen – sports day is rained off or the swimming pool is closed. A surprise 'mystery' '?' symbol can be used as a way of a getting pupils used to unexpected or unscheduled events, such as a fire drill.

The use of a schedule to structure a day or even just a lesson significantly reduces a pupil's anxiety and improves behaviour. The rule of thumb is the more anxious the pupil, the greater the degree of visual structure necessary. As the pupil grows in confidence in the classroom, so the level of visual structure can be diminished. Equally, should a pupil's anxiety increase for any reason, the level of visual structure will also need to be increased.

Gradual change

For pupils with SEND who find changes and new, uncertain, situations difficult to manage, gradual change strategies implemented over time will help develop a tolerance of change by gradually altering the minor aspects of a situation, event or activity, one step at a time. It is vital that the changes are made predictable for the pupil by using visual cues, such as a symbol schedule. The changes can then be increased as the child builds up some tolerance of uncertainty. When you tell pupils about a future event or activity that you cannot guarantee absolutely, such as 'Next Wednesday is sports day' this uncertainty should be made clear by adding 'probably', 'maybe' or 'we hope that'.

Moving from and into special schools

An increasing number of children now start their education in a special school and later transfer to a mainstream secondary school, and vice versa; or have dual placements, spending part of the week in mainstream and the remainder in a special school or resource base. For a child with more significant learning difficulties who may be more used to a small class with a high level of adult support, these transitions will be a huge step. In these situations a gradual integration into the new school is more appropriate.

A planned gradual transfer is the most effective way of developing successful inclusion. The transfer is a big event for the child with SEND and for the teachers, but that is also the case for the other pupils in the schools. In mainstream schools the impact on the other pupils can be overlooked in the concern to get the curriculum and access issues right. Suddenly to have a new pupil in class who may look different, act differently and who is treated differently – not to mention a possible new member of support staff – is a lot to expect the class to assimilate immediately.

Make as positive as possible those first contacts between the pupil with SEND and the rest of the groups they join. Plan the first visits to coincide with a less academic event, such as a dance festival, sports day or a Christmas fair. Praise the other pupils for their friendly behaviour and for being helpful. Explain that this new child is to join some of their lessons and that you want their help in planning a special welcome.

Very close liaison with the parents, the other teachers and the support agencies and therapists is an important part of the transition process. This co-operation often has very positive spin-offs, with joint projects and topics and expertise being shared between the two schools.

Preparing for adulthood

It is interesting that Chapter 8 of the SEND Code of Practice (2015) has the title 'Preparing for adulthood from the earliest years'. The Code of Practice defines preparing for adulthood as preparing children and young people for:

- higher education or employment;
- independent living arrangements, including supported living;
- participating in society;
- participating in, and contributing to, the local community;
- being as healthy as possible in adult life.

(7.38, p. 122)

Clearly, the expectation is that schools will begin this preparation well before Year 9 and the focus on aspirations and outcomes that underpin this. The process of looking forward to adulthood through aspirations, and then identifying the outcomes the child or young person needs to achieve by the end of the next key stage or phase of education to reach those aspirations, is embedded throughout the SEND reforms. All professionals working with and for children and young people with SEND need to listen to and acknowledge pupils' ambitions for the future. They must also have high expectations of what they can and will achieve. The professionals should focus on the child or young person's strengths and capabilities, in addition to their special educational and other needs. Thinking of these 'needs' as barriers to a pupil's learning and achievement makes it easier to decide what the school, college, or service should do to help their pupils overcome the barriers. High aspirations will look beyond academic achievement into employment, independent living and the child's full participation in the child or young person's community.

The aspirations of pupils with SEND must inform the development of the curriculum and extra-curricular opportunities. Successful schools will be those working in partnership with local business, other agencies and voluntary sector organisations to develop these opportunities, and to help pupils understand what is available to them as they get older, and what it is possible for them to achieve.

The intention is to give children and young people increasing choice, and control and freedom over their lives as they get older. This choice and control extends to their education, the support they receive, the work they do, and where and how they live. It will involve schools in supporting children and young people to develop strong friendships and other relationships, and giving them opportunities to explore different options for training and employment.

In many schools these additional expectations will be nothing new, and these schools will have person-centred approaches and systems in place on which to build. They will already have listened to and understood the interests, strengths and motivations of their pupils with SEND, and used this information to plan high quality support and provision around them. Other schools will have different starting points, and will need to develop the skills of person-centred planning and approaches to work effectively with young people with SEND and their families. A good starting point would be to work with local organisations for disabled people, and to enable pupils to get to know adults who are disabled and who are successful in work, sport or the arts, or who make a significant contribution to their own community.

Making decisions

A key aspect of preparing children and young people for adulthood is for them to begin to be, and to be enabled to be, involved in and make their own decisions about their own future – their education, their social life and, increasingly, the provision made for them and the support they receive. For many pupils with SEND, this will be a natural development, but others will need frequent opportunities (especially through secondary school) to make decisions for themselves, and to take on as much control of their own lives as possible.

Pupils with SEND often have fewer opportunities to make their own decisions than do other pupils, particularly if they have a high level of adult support. It is not uncommon to see a teaching assistant choose where a pupil will sit and which pen he or she should use, or even carrying the pupil's bag!

When pupils reach the end of compulsory school age (that is, the end of the academic year in which they turn 16), under the Children and Families Act 2014 the right to make their own decisions applies to them directly, rather than to their parents. That isn't to say that parents should have no part in supporting their son or daughter when important decisions have to be made, but the young person must be happy for them to do so, and the final decisions rest with the young person.

Transition into further education, training and employment

Preparing for adulthood reviews

High quality and effective preparation for adulthood is essential for all pupils with SEND, whether or not they have an EHC plan. It is perhaps even more important for pupils without EHC plans because there is no statutory mechanism on which to base the planning. All the elements of preparing for adulthood outlined below are relevant for pupils in receipt of SEN Support, and can be used as starting points for discussions with pupils and their parents.

From Year 9, all annual reviews of EHC plans will have planning for transition as the main focus. Discussions about a pupil's future should focus on what he or she wants to achieve, and the best way to support the reaching of that achievement. Planning for preparation for adulthood must be built into the revised EHC plan, and include a consideration of what post-16 options will be right for the individual pupil.

The planning process starts with an agreement on ambitious outcomes which focus on what the pupil wants for his or her future, and what he or she needs to be able to do by the end of the key stage to achieve these aspirations.

To prepare pupils for adulthood, planning in reviews of EHC plans should include:

- Identification of what provision needs to be put in place to prepare the pupil for further or higher education, training or employment. This will include:

  - Identifying appropriate post-16 pathways and opportunities that will enable pupils to achieve their outcomes. These post-16 pathways include training options such as supported internships, apprenticeships and traineeships, and support to help pupils to find and keep jobs, such as work experience or an employment mentor.

- Agreement of the support required to enable the pupil to live independently, including identification of what decisions the pupil wants to make for him or herself, and how they will make their own decisions as they become older.

  - This will include: where the pupil wants to live in the future, who he or she would prefer to live with, and what support is likely to be needed in order to achieve these preferences.

- Identification of what support the pupil will need to stay healthy in adult life, including the planning with health services around the transition from specialist children's services to adult health care. The age at which this transition to adult services happens can vary, so it is important that the pupil and his or her family understand when this will happen for them.
- Consideration of how the pupil will be helped to participate in the local and wider community. This will include finding solutions to issues such as mobility, transport, involvement in social activities, and developing and maintaining friendships and relationships.

(SEND Code of Practice, 2015, 8.10, pp. 125–126)

The documentation from the preparing for adulthood review and the subsequent revisions to the plan must be absolutely clear and specific about the support the young person needs to achieve his or her aspirations. It must also identify how the pupil will have the increasing choice, control and decision-making about his or her own support – how that support will be made available and who will provide it.

Moving from school to college or work

The final transition from school should be a celebration of shared experiences, successes and friendships. By the end of Year 11, a student should have forged lasting memories, and will feel secure and accepted by everyone in the school. Yet the true success of the student's time at the school will really be measured by how well they manage the move to further education, training or a job, just as much as the qualifications they gain. The five years of a secondary school career should be focused on preparing the student for the next stage of their lives. But it is a fine balance: give too much support and the student will become dependent; give too little or the wrong support and the student won't have the skills necessary to move forward. Remember that it is most unlikely a student will have the same level of adult support in further education as they have had in school – and they will certainly need to be independent in order to hold down a job.

Any next placement should have been decided months before a student reaches the end of Year 11 and he or she or she should have made numerous visits and be very familiar with the college or workplace. All the logistics of the new college or workplace need to be worked out and organised.

- How will the student get there?
- Who will meet him or her?
- Are the toilets accessible?
- What will he or she need to take?
- What happens on days when he or she has no lessons?
- Who can the student talk to if they are upset or anxious?

These might appear to be trivial issues, but it is this very kind of trivia that can cause tremendous anxiety for students and their families unless resolved. Specialist training for independence, such as in travel training or personal care, will help students to do as much for themselves as possible and will make them feel more confident in college or work.

Summary

All children and young people have to move through major changes and transitions throughout secondary school and into further education, training or employment. We cannot avoid these changes and transitions for pupils with SEND, but we can ease their way, and we must prepare them to manage and eventually to flourish in the adult world. Whatever steps schools take to help pupils with SEND through transitions will also help other students who may be less confident, or who have other difficulties in their lives. The reasonable adjustments made for one pupil will 'clear the ramp' for all the others.

Appendix

Inclusive teaching and learning checklist

School _____

Year/class _____

Teacher _____

Support staff/other adults in class _____

Number in class _____

Number of pupils receiving SEN Support _____

	Inclusive teaching	1 to 5	Impact/Even better if. . . .
1	Class or subject teacher takes full responsibility for the learning and behaviour of all pupils in the class.		
2	Lesson planning is in place showing differentiated activities and outcomes for all pupils in class.		
3	Lesson planning shows the role and expectations of any teaching assistants or other adults working with pupils during the lesson.		
4	Evidence of teacher and teaching assistant or other adults having jointly planned lesson activities and expected outcomes.		
5	Individual targets used to inform teaching and learning strategies and deployment of support.		
6	Differentiated learning resources ready and available at start of lesson.		
7	Classroom seating and layout planned well and clear of any obstacles.		

continued overleaf . . .

Inclusive teaching	I to 5	Impact/Even better if. . . .

8   Teacher welcomes all pupils into the room and settles class effectively so all are ready to learn.

9   Teacher introduces the lesson effectively giving pupils the 'big picture' and explaining where the learning fits into previous lessons and 'what comes next'.

10   Links to previous learning made explicit.

11   Variety of pairs and groups used effectively to support learning and cooperation.

12   Key vocabulary for lesson/subject displayed and available in required modes, i.e. on coloured paper, symbols, etc.

13   Lesson objectives displayed and explained to pupils at start of lesson.

14   Teacher checks all pupils are clear about the lesson structure and objectives.

15   Teacher refers back to lesson objectives at key points throughout the lesson.

16   Teacher works with all pupils at some point in the lesson.

17   Regular mini-plenaries used to maintain pace and monitor/assess understanding and learning.

18   The teacher monitors the learning of pupils working in small groups or 1–1 with a teaching assistant or other adult, including those working outside the classroom.

19   Questioning is carefully planned to include and challenge all pupils.

20   Pupils are given thinking/processing time before being required to respond to questions.

21   Alternatives to putting hands up or giving verbal responses made available.

22   Pupils are given opportunities and time to help each other.

23   Evidence of pupils being given pre-tutoring or follow-up support for learning.

24   Activities and tasks explained clearly or modeled.

25   Transitions between activities clearly signaled and managed well.

continued overleaf . . .

Inclusive teaching	1 to 5	Impact/Even better if. . . .
26 Instructional scaffolding used effectively for group and individual activities to support learning of all pupils.		
27 Alternatives to pen and paper tasks used.		
28 Effective use of IT is made to support learning and recording.		
29 Key parts of the lesson are presented in differing ways to maintain engagement and motivation.		
30 All adults provide pupils with positive verbal and written feedback on their learning.		
31 Additional adults observe learning and provide teacher with formative assessments on progress of all pupils.		
32 Peer assessment is used and managed effectively to support learning and progress.		
33 Good, appropriate behaviour is noticed and rewarded to support motivation and engagement.		
34 School behaviour policy implemented consistently throughout lesson.		
35 Homework tasks and expectations are well differentiated so that all pupils are able to complete and succeed in the activity.		

Evaluation

What were the positives in the lesson?

How could it be improved?

Priorities and next steps

References and suggested further reading

Alton, S., Beadman, J., Black, B., Lorenz, S. and McKinnon, C. (2003) *Education Support Pack for Schools*. London: Down's Syndrome Association.

Aronson, E. and Patnoe, S. (2011) *Cooperation in the Classroom: The jigsaw method*. London: Pinter & Martin.

Black, P., Harrison, C., Lee, C., Marshall, B. and Wiliam, D. (2004) Working inside the black box: assessment for learning in the classroom. *Phi Delta Kappan*, 86(1): 8–21.

Blatchford, P., Russell, A. and Webster, R. (2012) *Reassessing the Impact of Teaching Assistants: How research challenges policy and practice*. London: Routledge.

Blatchford, P., Bassett, P., Brown, P. and Webster, R. (2009) The effect of support staff on pupil engagement and individual attention. *British Educational Research Journal*, 35(5): 661–686.

Blatchford, P., Bassett, P., Brown, P., Martin, C., Russell, A. and Webster, R. (2009) The Deployment and Impact of Support Staff Project: Research brief (DCSF-RB148). London: Department for Children, Schools and Families.

Blatchford, P., Bassett, P., Brown, P., Martin, C., Russell, A. and Webster, R. (2011) The impact of support staff on pupils' positive approaches to learning and their academic progress. *British Educational Journal*, 37(3): 443–464, June.

Booth, T., Ainscow, M., Black-Hawkins, K., Vaughan, M. and Shaw, L. (2011) *Index for Inclusion: Developing learning and participation in schools* (3rd edn). Bristol: Centre for Inclusive Education (CSIE).

Buzan, T. (2010) *The Mind Map Book: Unlock your creativity, boost your memory, change your life*. London: Pearson.

Catsambis, S. (2001). Expanding knowledge of parental involvement in children's secondary education: connections with high school seniors' academic success. *Social Psychology of Education*, 5: 149–177.

Cheminais, R. (2014) *Special Educational Needs for Qualified and Trainee Teachers: A practical guide to the new changes* (3rd edn). London: Routledge.

Children and Families Act (2014) Chapter 6, Part 3, London: The Stationery Office.

Council for Disabled Children (2013) *Early Support School Age Developmental Journal*. London: National Children's Bureau.

Crozier, G. and Davies, J. (2007) Hard to reach parents or hard to reach schools? A discussion of home-school relations, with particular reference to Bangladeshi and Pakistani parents. *British Educational Research Journal*, 33(3): 295–313.

De Fraja, G., Oliveira, T. and Zanchi, L. (2010) Must try harder: Evaluating the role of effort in educational attainment. *The Review of Economics and Statistics*, 92(3): 577–597.

De Gaetano, Y. (2007) The role of culture in engaging Latino parents' involvement in school. *Urban Education*, 42(2): 145.

Department for Education (2010) *The Equality Act 2010 and Schools Departmental Advice for School Leaders, School Staff, Governing Bodies and Local Authorities*. London: Department for Education.

Department for Education (2011, updated 2013) *Teachers' Standards: Guidance for school leaders, school staff and governing bodies*. London: Department for Education.

Department for Education (2014) *Performance – P Scale – Attainment Targets for Pupils*. London: Department for Education.

Department for Education (2014, updated 2015) *Special Educational Needs and Disability Code of Practice: 0 to 25 years*. London: Department for Education.

Desforges, C. and Abouchaar, A. (2003) The impact of parental involvement, parental support and family education on pupil achievement and adjustment: A literature review research report. London: Department for Children, Schools and Families.

Doyle, M. B. and Giangreco, M. F. (2013) Guiding principles for including high school students with intellectual disabilities in general education classes. *American Secondary Education*, 42(1): 57–72.

Florez, M. T. and Sammons, P. (2013) *Assessment for Learning: Effects and impact*. Oxford University, Department of Education. CfBT Education Trust, pp. 3–4).

Giangreco, M. F. (2000) *Teaching Old Logs New Tricks: More absurdities and realities of education*. Minnetonka, MN: Peytral Publications.

Giangreco, M. F. (2003) Working with paraprofessionals. *Educational Leadership*, 61(2): 50–53.

Giangreco, M. F., Cloninger, C. J. and Iverson, V. S. (1998) *Choosing Outcomes and Accommodations for Children (COACH): A guide to educational planning for students with disabilities*. Baltimore, MD: Paul H. Brookes Publishing.

Goodall, J. and Vorhaus, J. (2011) *Review of Best Practice in Parental Engagement*. London: Department for Education.

Grayson, H. (2013) *Rapid Review of Parental Engagement and Narrowing the Gap in Attainment for Disadvantaged Children*. Slough and Oxford: NFER and Oxford University Press.

Greenhough, P., Hughes, M., Andrews, J., Goldstein, H., McNess, E., Osborn, M., Pollard, A., Stinchcombe, V. and Yee, W. S. (2007) What effect does involving parents in knowledge exchange activities during transfer from Key Stage 2 to Key Stage 3 have on children's attainment and learning dispositions? Paper presented at the British Educational Research Association Annual Conference, Institute of Education, University of London, 5–8 September.

Grove, N. and Walker, M. (1990) The Makaton vocabulary: using manual signs and graphic signals to develop interpersonal communication. *Augmentative and Alternative Communication*, 6: 15–28.

Harris, A. and Goodall, J. S. (2009) *Helping Families Support Children's Success at School*. Other: Save the Children.

Humphrey, N. and Squires, G. (2011) *Achievement for All: National evaluation*. London: Department for Education.

Jones, G. (2002) *Educational Provision for Children with Autism and Asperger Syndrome*. London: David Fulton Publishers.

Lamb, B. (2009) *Report of the Inquiry into Special Educational Needs and Parental Confidence*. Nottingham: DCSF Publications.

Lewis, A. L. (2002) Accessing, through research interviews, the views of children with difficulties in learning. *Support for Learning*, 17(3): 110–116.

Lewis, A. L, Davison, I. W., Ellins, J. L., Niblett, L., Parsons, S., Robertson, C. M. L. and Sharpe, J. (2007) The experiences of disabled pupils and their families. *British Journal of Special Education*, 34(4): 189–195.

National Strategies (2009) *Achievement for All: Guidance for schools*. London: Department for Children, Schools and Families.

National Strategies (2009) *Achievement for All: The Structured Conversation: Handbook to support training*. London: Department for Children, Schools and Families.

Newton, C. and Wilson, D. (2003) *Creating Circles of Friends: A peer support and inclusion workbook*. Nottingham. Inclusive Solutions.

Office for Standards in Education (2006) *Inclusion: Does it matter where pupils are taught? Provision and outcomes in different settings for pupils with learning difficulties and disabilities.* London: Ofsted.

Office for Standards in Education (2014) *School Inspection Handbook.* London: Ofsted.

Park, K. (2003) A voice and a choice. *Special Children*, 153: 30–31, February/March.

Park, K. (2003) How do objects become objects of reference? A review of the literature on objects of reference and a proposed model for the use of objects in communication. *British Journal of Special Education*, 24(3): 108–114.

Powell, G. (1999) *Current Research Findings to Support the Use of Signs with Adults and Children who have Intellectual and Communication Difficulties.* London: Makaton.

Russell, A., Webster, R. and Blatchford, P. (2013) *Maximising the Impact of Teaching Assistants: Guidance for school leaders and teachers.* London: Routledge.

Sainsbury, C. (2009) *Martian in the Playground: Understanding the schoolchild with Asperger's syndrome.* London. Lucky Duck Books (Sage).

Sherbert Research (2009) Parents as partners – 'Harder to engage' parents: qualitative research. London, Department for Children, Schools and Families.

United Nations (1990) *Convention on the Rights of the Child*, Office of the United Nations High Commissioner for Human Rights (OHCHR). Geneva, Switzerland.

Index

Printed in Great Britain
by Amazon

14128110R00106